'This is a wonderful project.  depressed, one of the great b: to my recovery – was the belie recover. I asked my doctor if with people who had recovered, so I could believe in it – but he couldn't and didn't. I think it would have made an enormous difference to me to know that it was possible to get better because, as Oscar Wilde said, "despair has no seasons" – in other words it is relentless. I thoroughly commend this book to any sufferers from depression. It contains messages of hope from the dark side, an antidote of rational belief to fight the lack of faith all depressives feel. *The Recovery Letters*, I have no doubt, has the power to save lives.'

– Tim Lott, journalist and author

'This book will save lives, which can't be said of many. Writing or reading a letter strikes at the sense of isolation which is at the root of despair. Read this book, buy it for others; it's rare and powerful medication.'

– Gwyneth Lewis, author of Sunbathing in the
Rain: A Cheerful Book about Depression

'These letters are full of friendship and intimacy. By pulling you out of yourself, they will help you to share the pain, test your perspective, and solve problems. It is possible to mend your way out of depression, and, believe me, you'll be all the better for it: more thoughtful, more receptive, and more at peace.'

– Dr Neel Burton, author of Growing from Depression

'I found the letters so helpful when I was ill; one of the few things that reached me across the void.'
— *Charlotte Garrett, research psychologist*

'Powerful letters from people who've been there who know from experience that you won't always feel this way. Just one letter that really speaks to you could make a difference.'
— *Claudia Hammond, broadcaster and writer*

'Moving, beautiful in places and valuable: in a world in which effective treatment for the mentally ill remains as elusive as ever, this book has something rather important to offer. More than anything, the depression sufferer wants reassurance that recovery is possible. These letters from fellow travellers show that it is not just possible, but probable, that you are not alone, that others have been here, survived, recovered, rejoined their lives. Their message: you can do the same.'
— *Mark Rice-Oxley, author of* Underneath the Lemon Tree: A Memoir of Depression and Recovery

'This collection of letters from those in depression recovery will no doubt give solace to those currently suffering from mental illness. The people writing these letters describe depression in a way that only survivors can. The words are authentic and will give hope and encouragement to those who read them.'
— *Douglas Bloch MA, author of* Healing from Depression: 12 Weeks to a Better Mood

The Recovery Letters

of related interest

We're All Mad Here
The No-Nonsense Guide to Living with Social Anxiety
Claire Eastham
Foreword by Natasha Devon, MBE
ISBN 978 1 78592 082 0
eISBN 978 1 78450 343 7

Can I tell you about Depression?
A guide for friends, family and professionals
Christopher Dowrick and Susan Martin
Illustrated by Mike Medaglia
ISBN 978 1 84905 563 5
eISBN 978 1 78450 003 0

Recovery from Depression Using the Narrative Approach
A Guide for Doctors, Complementary Therapists
and Mental Health Professionals
Damien Ridge
ISBN 978 1 84310 575 6
eISBN 978 1 84642 878 4

The Madness of Our Lives
Experiences of Mental Breakdown and Recovery
Penny Gray
ISBN 978 1 84310 057 7
eISBN 978 1 84642 504 2

The Recovery Letters

Addressed to People Experiencing Depression

Edited by James Withey
and Olivia Sagan

Afterword by G. Thomas Couser

Jessica Kingsley *Publishers*
London and Philadelphia

First published in 2017
by Jessica Kingsley Publishers
73 Collier Street
London N1 9BE, UK
and
400 Market Street, Suite 400
Philadelphia, PA 19106, USA

www.jkp.com

Library of Congress Cataloging in Publication Data
Names: Withey, James, editor. | Sagan, Olivia, editor..
Title: The recovery letters : addressed to people experiencing
depression /
  edited by James Withey and Olivia Sagan.
Description: London ; Philadelphia : Jessica Kingsley Publishers, 2017.
Identifiers: LCCN 2017014424 (print) | LCCN 2017005944 (ebook) | ISBN
  9781784504601 (ebook) | ISBN 9781785921834 (alk. paper)
Subjects: LCSH: Depression, Mental--Alternative treatment. |
Narrative
  therapy.
Classification: LCC RC537 (print) | LCC RC537 .R4236 2017 (ebook) |
DDC
  616.85/27--dc23

British Library Cataloguing in Publication Data
A CIP catalogue record for this book is available from the British
Library

ISBN 978 1 78592 183 4
eISBN 978 1 78450 460 1

Printed and bound in Great Britain

CONTENTS

· · · · · · · · · · · · · · · · · · · ·

Acknowledgements   **8**

Introduction: Why I Started The Recovery Letters   **9**
James Withey

Introduction: Writing Letters: A Subtle Therapy   **18**
Olivia Sagan

The Letters   **27**

Afterword: There's Life in Letters   **227**
G. Thomas Couser

· · · · · · · · · · · · · · · · · · · ·

ACKNOWLEDGEMENTS

My biggest thank you is to the letter writers, for your courage to write, to be vulnerable, to be hopeful and to share your story to help others.

Thank you to Maytree, Sanctuary for the Suicidal in London, UK. Thank you to the staff and volunteers during my stay who saw a man crushed but not annihilated, who sat with me when I didn't want to sit by myself, who believed I could live when all I wanted was to die. In particular, thank you to Roz.

Thank you to everyone from BBC Radio 4's 'All in the Mind' programme, who saw what we were doing at The Recovery Letters, believed in it and invited me to speak about it.

Thank you to Olivia for your support and for believing, like me, that this should be a book.

Thank you to my family and friends; you know who you are and what you've done. Thank you for standing by me.

As always, thank you to Patrick, my Huckleberry friend.

James Withey

WHY I STARTED THE RECOVERY LETTERS

James Withey

I've always loved letters; writing them and receiving them. As a child I would write to pen friends from around the world. I adored the physical act of opening up the letter, smelling the paper and imagining the sender with their pen and their thoughts in a different part of the world.

The best letters touch your soul. They reach out to you; they take hold of the part of you that feels alone and make you cry out, 'Me too! I thought it was just me, but you understand this as well.' I hope that's what this collection of letters will do: connect to the part of you that feels you are the only one suffering from depression.

Letters, in whatever format they come in, are something to treasure, to re-read and keep. There is nothing more personal; the person has sat down and thought about you and only you, and now here you are, reading that they care.

A few years ago I was sat on my bed, in my room, in a psychiatric hospital. The bed was bolted to the floor, the window only opened two inches and it looked like the rubbish bin had been set on fire at some point. Every so often someone would come along, look through the glass in the door, see that I was alive and go away again.

At 3 o'clock in the afternoon the sun would start to project the shadows of the tree across the wall in a ridiculously incongruous display. I looked at the beauty and it barely touched me. I kept thinking, 'How did I end up here? How did this happen? How did depression do this to me? How did my belt get taken away from me? How did I end up promising never to have a plastic bag in the room?' Again, again and again, 'How did I end up here?' The previous year, I was working as a staff trainer in a large charity and teaching suicide prevention; now, I'm on 15-minute suicide watch.

What I didn't know in hospital was that I would start developing the idea for The Recovery Letters project, which has changed my life and changed other people's too. A project so simple and with hope at its heart.

During the severest part of my depression all I could think about was suicide. I would wake up crying at 4.30am and I couldn't get back to sleep. On the train home from work I looked out of the window and made plans; Thursday, yes Thursday I would kill myself, it's going to be Thursday. I would walk in front of a train and the pain would be gone. That's all that mattered, getting rid of the pain.

If I had taken a bath by 4pm this was a good day. If I had eaten something this would feel like an unwanted achievement. I would go to the supermarket with a list of things to buy and stand in front of the aisles and think, 'How did I used to do this?' What sort of tuna should I buy? The cheap one as I had little money? The one with spring water as I had been told brine contained mercury? The more expensive one where I might get more fish for my money? A multi-pack on offer? Did the one with the olive oil preserve the tuna better? It was impossible. One decision led to another, more questioning, more agony. More than once I walked out of the supermarket with nothing. The music was too loud, people seemed to be running down the aisles towards me, there were screaming babies and harsh tannoy announcements. It was hell in my hell.

I couldn't concentrate, I couldn't watch television, I paced around our flat and resented every sunny day, every person who tried to smile at me at the post office, but most of all I resented myself. This was all my fault. When I told people I was suffering with depression they were shocked. I had been the person who always listened to their problems and here I was, incapable of looking after myself.

Depression is about loss and there were many losses in my life during this time; relationships with friends were permanently altered, I couldn't work, I couldn't concentrate, I couldn't exercise, I didn't want to eat, I couldn't sleep, I lost all hope and, most significantly for me, I couldn't read.

Reading novels was my joy. I joined book groups, read a few novels a month, spent my time in old book shops, read online book reviews, scored and recorded my favourite books in a special journal, and lunch times were spent reading my book. Now, I couldn't read a sentence. Nothing; it was extraordinary in its totality. People would recommend tombstone-like books on depression and cognitive behavioural therapy (CBT) and they sat on the coffee table staring at me. I stared back, bemused. How did I used to do this? I used to just pick up a book and read the words, and now, nothing. Nothing. Just nothing.

One of the many cruelties of depression is that it takes away your coping mechanisms just when you need them and then convinces you they will never come back and it's all your fault anyway. At your lowest point, when you need all your resources, depression takes them away.

I never thought I would get any better, never, ever, ever. 'It may happen to other people...' I said, '...but not for me.' If I was ever convinced of anything in my life, it was that my depression would not improve. I would have placed significant bets on this had the local bookmaker accepted my odds; I would have been immensely rich and permanently depressed. I was wrong – it did get better and now I do my best not to listen too much when depression starts to tell me similar lies; it doesn't always work but I try and that's all we can do, try and not listen to the lies.

Depression is a life-threatening, sometimes life-taking illness that takes huge guts to live with. The level of emotional pain is so huge that suicide can seem like the only option. It's also a devious cuckoo taking over your life, spitting and berating you with lies, hate and blame. It's hideous. It makes you believe the temporary is permanent and that you can never recover. The biggest mental health stigma is our own; and its fuel is depression.

When I was first unwell only one mental health worker ever told me I could recover from depression; they were a student with the crisis team who would visit me every day to see if I was alive. As they were leaving they turned in the doorway and said, 'James, it is possible to recover from depression.' It was possible to recover from depression? Really? But the problem was, depression was telling me the opposite and in the loudest voice it had. I thought it was impossible, I would never get better, it was hopeless, living was pointless, the pain was too much and that it was more powerful than everything, just give up. But that day there was a tiny chink of hope and I realised that I needed to hear more about the possibilities of recovery if I was ever going to get any better.

I went to stay at Maytree Respite Centre in London (a residential service for people actively suicidal) and more hope was let in. I was able to speak freely about wanting to die; they listened, they understood, they saw the pain and saw me in the middle of the pain. They didn't panic and want to rescue me; they sat with me, literally and metaphorically. 'I feel destroyed,' I said. 'The very essence of me has been annihilated, how can I continue when there is nothing left of me?'

'I don't see that...' said the worker, 'I see a man who has been crushed but not annihilated.'

And then something inside me changed, some small light came on, it was flickering and fragile but definitely there. Maybe there was something of me left?

Alongside my own recovery the idea of The Recovery Letters started to gather momentum. What if people who were recovering from depression wrote to those that were currently suffering? What if people could read that recovery was possible? What if these letters could reach out to the small part of them that wanted to believe in recovery? What if they acted as small shots of hope? What if they helped people see that they weren't alone?

When I got out of the psychiatric hospital I started a blog and wrote the first Recovery Letter; it's here in the book: 'From James'. I started a Twitter account (@RecoveryLetters) and asked other people to write letters and things started to grow. Such a simple idea seemed to be helping people, and the letter writers gained as much from the writing as the readers.

Recovery is not the same as 'recovered'. Recovery is about trying to live with depression, it's about trying to find meaning in what you do, trying to see the future, trying to get to work, to get the kids in bed, to fix the car and trying not to scream when the bin bag splits and the rubbish goes all over the kitchen floor. It's about trying and about doing the best you can. Symptoms can lessen, the pain can subside, meaning can return, happiness can enter in again and maybe, just maybe, there might be moments of utter, rapturous joy. Recovery is about starting to see the 'point' when we say to ourselves, 'What's the point?'

I tried many things to feel better: I cycled, tried mindfulness meditation, volunteered in an allotment, went to a depression self-help group, went on retreat to a monastery, found some decent low-cost counselling, tried cognitive behavioural therapy, watched soothing television and terrible television, but mostly I did nothing. I rested; I had to, my soul needed to heal.

I am not better. I won't ever be 'better' because better doesn't exist and as soon as I realised that I started to live with less pressure. I will live with depression for the rest of my life. We will bicker and fight, I will get resentful and depression will try and take me under, but also strangely I will be grateful to it, because as much as depression has taken away it has also given. It has made me a different person, I prioritise myself now, I do things I wouldn't have done before.

Do I wish that I didn't have depression? Absolutely; every single moment of every single day, but wishing won't take it away and only acceptance moves me forward.

We share stories of depression to help others, to help ourselves and because the more we write and talk and share our experiences, the more it weakens depression. Our stories are so important because depression tells us we're not worthy of life let alone speech. So, we have to talk and write as much as we can.

This book is about giving you testimonies, from the people who know that recovery is possible. The writers of these letters come from all over the world and experience all types of depression: bipolar, postpartum depression and major/clinical depression. Their letters don't disguise how painful depression is but they simply and beautifully say that it won't always feel that way. It's worth writing that again...it won't always feel that way.

They are writing to you because they know that hope is absent with depression; their letters will help your own hope grow. And it will. It really will. Some of these letters will appeal more than others, that's okay, we've tried to ensure that there are a variety to choose from. Also, you don't need to read this book in a traditional way – flick through the pages and find a letter that appeals; I strongly believe there are letters in here that will help because they've helped me too. Some may trigger thoughts you may not want because the letters don't hide how painful depression is. Some might offer advice based on what's worked for them – try the bits that you want to, see what works; recovery is an ongoing box of tools to keep trying.

Please look after yourself and keep remembering that these letters are written to YOU from people who are recovering and, as one of the letter writers says, we're all rooting for you.

In between the letters we have included some quotes about depression that I've written. If your concentration gets really bad we hope these small lines will help until you can read the letters.

If you've been helped and inspired by these letters you may want to write a letter of your own; visit www.therecoveryletters.com for all the details and we look forward to hearing from you

This is a book to keep with you; let it accompany you, tuck it into the glove box, pop it into your bag when you go on holiday, have it by your bed for when you wake up at 4 o'clock in the morning.

When important passages arrive in books I now turn the page corner over; please do the same. This is a book to use; underline sentences that mean something to you, circle passages with your favourite pen, mark the pages that you love; make it meaningful, make it yours.

This is your book.

James Withey

WRITING LETTERS: A SUBTLE THERAPY

Olivia Sagan

As a child, I already knew writing was a form of magic. Early scribbles morphed into small words that became longer and polysyllabic; sentences swelled to phrases and paragraphs; random thoughts transformed themselves into poems, stories, diary entries and letters: *Dear me* – when that me felt anything but dear.

Writing has been with me (and at times against me) as I have grown and negotiated sadness, loss, depression and confusion. It has been the simplest, yet most complex, of loyal companions. Later, as I worked as a counsellor it offered a tool to help others when things were unsayable; it gave a way forward when there was fear that a word spoken could never be retracted. I watched people write letters never to send them; write letters to instantly burn them; write letters to seal and to keep until a later date. For some people writing a letter to the injured party, the perpetrator, the lost loved one or the one yearned for, shifted them, ever so slightly, from inert and entrenched pain to the beginnings of a beyond. Letters, regardless of whether a recipient exists, regardless of whether they get sent or ever received, regardless of whether they are to ourselves or a part of ourselves, can start a loosening, like springtime in the fields, of the sod of our distress.

In the midst now of the 21st century, we are the stuff of the printed word as never before. Bombarded not daily but moment by moment through devices that are never switched off, words hit us and scatter, disseminated through newsfeeds, blogs, vlogs, ephemeral social networks, online forums and emails, attachments, the slick PDF, the soporific PowerPoint, the ebook. We still know writing is a form of magic, and we are perennially seduced by the alchemy. We are also soothed, lifted and consoled by writing's magic, and its therapeutic qualities have been the focus of many people's attention, for a long time (Greenhalgh & Hurwitz, 1998).

Writing has been shown to have a long history within mental health settings, even when the practice was frowned upon or outright prohibited. The poignant account by Gail Hornstein (2009) of Victorian-era asylum resident Agnes Richter, who painstakingly stitched an autobiographical text into every inch of a jacket she created from her institutional uniform, is but one testament to how people have turned, throughout time, to expressing their pain and distress in a written form, often overcoming formidable obstacles. Often, too, these words and writings had to be hidden, like those of Roseanne in the Sebastian Barry novel *The Secret Scripture* (2009), whose life story, written on scavenged paper, was kept under the floor boards in her asylum room.

Researchers have turned avid attention to the drive to express mental pain, with demonstrations of writing's therapeutic value (Bolton, 1997; DeSalvo, 1999; Harris, 2003; Hartill, 1998; Hunt, 2000; Lepore & Smyth, 2002; Philips, Linington & Penman, 1999; Smyth & Greenberg, 2000; Ullrich & Lutgendorf, 2002). James Pennebaker and his colleagues have carried out a number of well-known studies into the health benefits of writing, and report persuasive results (Graybeal, Sexton & Pennebaker, 2002; Pennebaker & Evans, 2014).

There has been a call for more use to be made of creative writing within healthcare settings and for the practice to be encouraged (Jones, 2003), with an emphasis on the importance for the writer of being able to write without having to please anyone (Wright, 2003). Writing can offer an important counterbalance of story; the things we 'know' about ourselves, our history, our depression and our pain are influenced by the dominant narratives of those more powerful than ourselves, particularly those in whose care we have been. The stories we develop about ourselves are often limiting, and derive from a social context. So the processes of 're-authoring', of being heard and of telling, are linked to ideas of personal empowerment and collective struggle

(Besley, 2002; McLeod, 1997), core tenets of the recovery movement (Neilsen & Murphy, 2008). Writing offers an identity other than the ill, the victim, the survivor, the patient. When we write, we are writers (King, Neilsen & White, 2013) and we may be able to shift our otherwise entrenched toxic narratives (Sagan, 2011).

Letter writing, as a practice apart from creative and autobiographical writing, has a long history, with some claiming letters to be the oldest form of literature (Dawson & Dawson, 1909). Some accounts cite the earliest epistle as that of Atossa, queen and daughter of Cyrus the Great, who lived from 550 BCE to 475 BCE. There is evidence of letters from the ancient world written on metal, on lead, on wax-coated wooden tablets, on animal skin and on papyrus. But there is little mention of letter writing as a therapeutic activity until the 20th century, when its popularity grew in great part as a result of the wider interest in writing's therapeutic value and its use in narrative therapy (White & Epston, 1990).

Narrative therapy could be considered something of a 'counter-therapy'. In its critiquing of traditional therapeutic practices and its positioning of therapy as inherently a political activity with a set of practices inscribed by power relations, narrative therapy seeks to re-empower the 'client', helping them re-author their lives. Letter writing has become an important part of narrative therapy (White & Epston, 1989, 1990), but is also theorised from a range of psychological perspectives (Jolly, 2011). It is used to map experience onto the temporal dimension and to help the writer re-evaluate experiences, and thus becomes a mechanism for understanding the meanings we ascribe to experiences. Letter writing in this context is also said to aid short-term memory, enabling people to be 'more active in determining the arrangement of information and experience, and in the production of different accounts of events and experience' (White & Epston, 1990, p.37). When sent, therapeutic letters impact not only on the writers, but on the recipients too (Wojcik & Iverson, 1989).

The internet has opened less of a door and more of a world of possibility for the writing of letters about our mental health, depression and recovery. Even a cursory search yields sites and items wherein people of all walks of life and ages choose the letter form as a means of externalising, empowering and re-scripting. It has already been suggested that 'perhaps email is the inevitable future of therapeutic letters' (Moules, 2009, p.109) and indeed, why not? Letter writing has shown itself to be resilient and flexible as an activity and the 21st century will no doubt be witness to the epistle's next form.

Why we continue to write these letters and emails is an interesting question, with a multifaceted answer that cannot here be fully explored. But some clues lie in the aforementioned therapeutic value and the cathartic experience; the sense of settling old scores, of fighting back, of reclaiming one's self or a part of that self, and of re-scripting, especially when your life feels to have slipped out of your own control. There is empowerment and retribution; the easing of an urge to externalise and 'a means to anchor new stories that promote personal agency' (Paré & Majchrzak Rombach, 2003, p.202). In his study of autobiographical medical narratives Aronson (2000) suggests the reasons for writing include people also wanting:

> to communicate with others in order to help them to understand what it is like to be a patient and to come to terms with their own illness, reasons that are often linked to the patient's own similar needs, both emotional and intellectual. These include a desire to remove the stigma associated with diseases such as depression or cancer. (p.1600)

He notes too that 'Reading patients' tales can help doctors understand their patients better and teach them things they won't learn from textbooks' (p.1599).

The letters in this volume are all written about depression and ways through and sometimes out of it. By reading them in no particular order we learn about depression, the forms and trajectories it takes, the stages of its tenure and textures, its horrors and demands. We read of people's slowly developed strategies, their personal toolbox contents, their mantras, go-tos and fallbacks: *Just keep breathing.* We read of bravery – the sheer grit and courage of keeping on keeping on.

The letters remain important 'historical' documents, whether real or virtual, about who someone is, their experiences, thoughts and feelings. Each letter is a window onto a person's interiority. Each opens a crack or vista of the otherwise closed, sometimes tight and intolerable spaces of the depression dungeon, the *'tent of blue'*. And each letter offers up how the individual relates to these spaces and states: negotiating them, rejecting, hating, railing against or learning to accept them. And as such we are privileged to read them, as the sharing of such processes with another is an act sometimes brave, sometimes therapeutic, sometimes bloody-minded, but invariably, at its core, generous.

So these letters are a unique and rare way of getting to know another person, and in so doing, finding a part of ourselves. As G. Thomas Couser in his afterword tells of getting to know his father through letters, I feel the reader will get to know a little about the writers of these letters and take heart, be inspired, be calmed, be angered and be motivated. In her article exploring the fate of handwritten letters in the 21st century Clare Brant (2006, p.17) claims that 'The twenty-first century shows epistolary archetypes are durable: the handwritten letter has lost none of its power to haunt.' I'll end on her words later on in her article:

> Letters stay powerful not because they can be read simplistically as personal, nor simply because of their survival for so long, but because they look to the future: they prove we are humans, not cyborgs.

Olivia Sagan

REFERENCES

Aronson, J. K. (2000). Autopathography: the patient's tale. *British Medical Journal, 321*(7276), 1599–1602.

Barry, S. (2009). *The Secret Scripture.* London: Penguin.

Bolton, G. (1997). *Writing Myself: The Therapeutic Potential of Creative Writing.* London: Jessica Kingsley Publishers.

Besley, A. C. (2002). Foucault and the turn to narrative therapy. *British Journal of Guidance and Counselling, 30*(2), 125–143.

Brant, C. (2006). Devouring time finds paper toughish: what's happened to handwritten letters in the twenty-first century? *a/b: Auto/Biography Studies, 21*(1), 7–19.

Dawson, W. J. & Dawson, C. W. (1909). *The Great English Letter-Writers* (Vol. 1). London: Hodder & Stoughton.

DeSalvo, L. (1999). *Writing as a Way of Healing: How Telling Our Stories Transforms Our Lives.* London: The Women's Press.

Graybeal, A., Sexton, J & Pennebaker, J. W. (2002). The role of story-making in disclosure writing: the psychometrics of narrative. *Psychology and Health, 17*(5), 571–581.

Greenhalgh, T. & Hurwitz, B. (1998). Why Study Narrative? In T. Greenhalgh & B. Hurwitz (eds) *Narrative Based Medicine: Dialogue and Discourse in Clinical Practice.* London: BMJ Books, pp.3–16.

Harris, J (2003). *Signifying Pain: Constructing and Healing the Self Through Writing.* Albany, NY: State University of New York Press.

Hartill, G. (1998). The Web of Words: Collaborative Writing and Mental Health. In C. Hunt & F. Sampson (eds) *The Self on the Page: Theory and Practice of Creative Writing in Personal Development.* London: Jessica Kingsley Publishers, pp.47–52.

Hornstein, G. (2009). *Agnes's Jacket: A Psychologist's Search for the Meanings of Madness.* New York: Rodale Press.

Hunt, C. (2000). *Therapeutic Dimensions of Autobiography in Creative Writing.* London: Jessica Kingsley Publishers.

Jolly, M. (2011). What I never wanted to tell you: therapeutic letter writing in cultural context. *Journal of Medical Humanities, 32*(1), 47–59.

Jones, A. (2003). Poetry, creative writing and therapy. *Healthcare Counselling and Psychotherapy Journal, 3*(3), 44–46.

King, R., Neilson, P. & White, E. (2013). Creative writing in recovery from severe mental illness. *International Journal of Mental Health Nursing, 22*(5), 444–452.

Lepore, S. J. & Smyth, J. M. (eds) (2002). *The Writing Cure: How Expressive Writing Promotes Health and Emotional Well-Being.* Washington, DC: American Psychological Society.

McLeod, J. (1997). *Narrative and Psychotherapy.* London: Sage.

Moules, N. J. (2009). The past and future of therapeutic letters: family suffering and healing words. *Journal of Family Nursing,* 15(1), 102–111.

Neilsen, P. & Murphy, F. (2008). The potential role of life-writing therapy in facilitating 'recovery' for those with mental illness. *M/C Journal,* 11(6). Retrieved from http://journal.media-culture. org.au/index.php/mcjournal/article/view/110, accessed on 10 February 2017.

Paré, D. A. & Majchrzak Rombach, M. A. (2003). Therapeutic Letters to Young Persons. In C. F. Sori & L. Hecker (eds) *The Therapists' Notebook for Children and Adolescents.* Binhampton, NY: Haworth Press, pp.199–203.

Pennebaker, J. & Evans, J. (2014). *Expressive Writing: Words That Heal.* Enumclaw, WA: Idyll Arbor.

Philips, D., Linington, L. & Penman, D. (1999). *Writing Well: Creative Writing and Mental Health.* London: Jessica Kingsely Publishers.

Sagan, O. (2011). Interminable knots: hostages to toxic stories. *Pedagogy, Culture and Society,* 19(1), 97–118.

Smyth, J. M. & Greenberg, M. A. (2000). Scriptotherapy: The Effects of Writing About Traumatic Events. In P. R. Duberstein & J. M. Masling (eds) *Psychodynamic Perspectives on Sickness and Health.* Washington, DC: American Psychological Association, pp.121–154.

Ullrich, P. M. & Lutgendorf, S. K. (2002). Journaling about stressful events: effects of cognitive processing and emotional expression. *Annals of Behavioral Medicine,* 24(3), 244–250.

White, M. & Epston, D. (1989). *Literate Means to Therapeutic Ends.* Adelaide: Dulwich Centre.

White, M. & Epston, D. (1990). *Narrative Means to Therapeutic Ends.* New York: W.W. Norton & Co.

Wojcik, J. V. & Iverson, E. R. (1989). Therapeutic letters: the power of the printed word. *Journal of Strategic and Systemic Therapies,* 8(2–3), 77–81.

Wright, J. (2003). 'Writing therapy' and research: stuck in the swamp between practice and…? *Journal of Critical Psychology, Counselling and Psychotherapy,* 31, 1–8.

THE LETTERS

✉

You aren't depression,
you're you
and the essence of
you hasn't gone.

FROM CLARE

Dear You,

Right now you probably don't think you'll ever feel better. The idea that anything could actually help seems ridiculous – a pointless hope. Friends don't understand why you genuinely can't see how you'll ever be happy again. It's as if you're in different worlds – or on different islands.

I'm writing from a happier island now. There's clear blue skies and sparkling sea. Of course it's dark, cold and miserable sometimes, but I can remember what the sun feels like here. I can imagine feeling happy even when times are hard.

But – if you're anything like me – your depressed island is not somewhere where the sun used to shine. It's always been swirling with a dark fog that reflects and magnifies negative thoughts until they suffocate you into submission.

When you're there it's as if you've been there forever. You forget that you've ever been happy. You forget what happiness feels like. And if you've forgotten that, how can you believe you'll feel it again? It's just a word with no emotional link in your mind.

It's hard to trust in something you can't feel. Trusting that there are things out there that will help – that you'll feel better in ways you can't imagine now – is enormously hard.

That's why you need messages from the sunnier island. Postcards to tell you that – somehow – you'll find yourself back there again. Letters to remind you of what helps.

So even if you don't believe you'll ever feel warmth on your skin again, try and be gentle with yourself. Depression often reverses our motivation. You have to start doing something in order to get a glimpse of how it can help.

It's not easy. Rationally you might know that getting out of the house will help but emotionally you've got nothing. But once you get going you'll slowly start to remember what a better mood feels like.

Exercise helps. Sleep well and drink less alcohol. Write things down and talk to people around you. Seek help when you need it and (hardest of all) trust that depression isn't all there ever was and all there ever will be. Better times exist, even if they feel lost in soupy fog right now.

And – when you're feeling well – write to yourself. Remind yourself how you feel when things are going well. Try and describe the positive and hopeful feelings, the things you take pleasure in and the things you are looking forward to. Recognise that your depressed self won't really be able to imagine any of these things but remind them that, like before, things have changed and improved. Remind them to hold on and to trust.

Doing that helps me work out how to spend most of my life in a place where I know what sunshine feels like. I hope it helps you too.

See you soon,

Clare

FROM ANDREW

Dear You,

If you are fighting depression and suicidal thoughts, you probably feel alone right now.

If you're anything like me, you probably feel scared, everything probably seems confusing and it probably seems like there is no hope of recovery. Maybe you feel lost, as if you don't know who you are or where you fit in the world. There's probably a part of you that feels angry at the illness and maybe even at yourself.

The thought of living each day is too hard, the idea of waking up tomorrow and going through it all again seems unbearable. There have been times where there seemed to be no escape, where suicide seemed the only option left, but we're both still here. We're still alive, we're still fighting, and we're still trying to make things better.

Listen to me: you've made it to today. You are allowed to feel proud of that.

When suicidal thoughts enter my head, they bring with them immense feelings of guilt and shame. You might look around at other people, other situations from across the world, and you might think, 'What have I got to feel bad about? All these other people have it so much worse than me, yet they can cope, they can be happy.' That's what it was like for me, and that's where the guilt and shame came from.

You have to stop comparing yourself with how you think other people are. It's hard when everyone seems happy, but you never know what people feel like in private. Comparing yourself to others is the worst thing you can do. Your situation is unique to you. It is NOT your fault that you haven't developed the ability to cope with particular situations. It is NOT your fault that you feel the way you feel. This whole situation is NOT your fault. You are poorly, that's all, and with support you will get well again, I promise.

Just keep breathing.

Depression left me feeling weak, both physically and mentally. It made me feel like a failure, but the truth is that nothing could be further from the truth. To have these thoughts, to be fighting against yourself and the urges depression makes you feel, to make it through the day while dealing with this illness, it's the strongest thing anybody can do, and you should be damn proud that you are here. You have strength and bravery beyond what you realise, and you demonstrate that every day, just by getting through to tomorrow.

You can get better. You will get better.

Just keep breathing.

If there's one thing you need to know, it's that you are not alone. You are never alone. You may think you are, but it's the illness telling you that, and it is lying to you. The truth is there are millions of us, all suffering variants of the same illness. The nature of that illness makes it harder to talk about it, but when we do, we strike the first blow to the demon of depression.

Please talk to someone.

You deserve to get better.

You deserve to be happy.

I believe you can get through this.

I believe you will get through this.

I believe in you.

Andrew

FROM MATT

....

Dear You,

I can empathise with how you feel. It's properly shit, isn't it?

I felt like that too a while ago and thought there was no escape which was a very scary and frightening experience, however, I got better and in time you will get better. There is much I could write to you but I really don't want to come across as insincere or pretend to have the answers so will keep it short.

What I learnt on the path that took me from depression, anxiety and grief to being myself again was humbling. A person I met who is now my good friend, also suffering at the time, said to me, 'Trust the journey.' It made me cry and weep with frustration but upon reflection I resolved to use it as a talisman in all I did, leaving the house, speaking to people, getting in the car, going back to work, going for a run, drawing a picture, walking the dog and just being quiet in a room on my own. I learnt to trust myself again and you will also.

The endless ways to describe the highs and lows of how we feel I can't summarise and others will do a better job at it, however, I hope that reading these words helps you to know there are many people who understand what you are going through and how you will come out the other side stronger in ways at present it is hard to imagine.

Yours,

Matt

FROM LORNA

Dear You,

Depression is not weakness. I don't expect you to believe that right now, it took me many years to believe it but it's true.

We all, no matter how strong, seem to have our limits. Having limits is not weakness, it's normal. We are humans not machines.

Once I finally accepted that I was not weak for feeling as I did, there was a glimmer of light. I wasn't useless, weak, pathetic or a waste of space.

Your glimmer of light may come from somewhere else, but I believe it will come.

I don't know how your depression is manifesting itself but I do know how frightening and disorientating the feelings it can generate can be.

You are not alone, though I suspect that it feels very much that way.

Depression is a great isolator. For me, that isolation intensified the horrific feelings. I reached out for help several times but it was many years before I received it, but the difference it has made is hard to describe.

I hope you are also able to find what it is you need to help you find your way again.

I will never meet you, hear from you or know your name but I walk beside you.

Take care.

Lorna

FROM MIRIAM

Dear You,

I am writing this letter to let you know that I am rooting for you.

Depression is debilitating. I know, because I went through it – twice. One of the worst feelings for me was that I would never recover and no matter how many times my friends and family would encourage me, I could not believe them. You might feel the same way. I am proof that one can emerge victorious from the depth of despair. It takes a lot of hard work – effort that I did not know was humanly possible. I literally put one foot in front of the other. People use that term loosely, but they have not a clue what it can really mean. People who are suffering or have suffered from depression, you, me, can appreciate its true definition.

There were a few keys in my recovery. One of the first actions I took was to create some structure for myself, to have somewhere to go in the morning. I volunteered at a school where I used to work. Although it did help me to recover, working there was one of the hardest things I have ever done in my life, namely because people there knew me from before and I was extremely self-conscious that they would discover something was amiss.

Exercise was another integral part of my schedule. Often, I would drag myself there, with my last ounce of motivation. Usually, afterwards I would feel both calmer and proud that I accomplished this feat. Of course, medication and therapy, specifically cognitive behavioural therapy, were forerunners in my recovery as well.

You may not be able to do all that I did and that is okay. Recovery takes time. At one point when I was becoming impatient with my progress, my psychiatrist told me that recovering from depression is like grass growing. In other words, it takes time. You may not be able to see grass growing, but the important thing is that it is.

You might still be at the stage of not wanting to get out of bed. Been there, done that. Recovery is a balance between pushing yourself and at the same time having patience and compassion for yourself. Surround yourself with supportive people. I was fortunate to have my parents as cheerleaders. Every time I would accomplish a challenge, like travelling a distance myself, my father would give me another notch on my belt. Till this day, we joke about it.

Right now, it might sound absurd, but one day, you might even embrace this overwhelming experience as a positive life-changing event that has made you a deeper, more compassionate human being who feels the world in a more nuanced, beautiful way.

I have experienced some of the challenges you are facing and it is possible to come out triumphant. When you are feeling discouraged, know that I am out there rooting for you.

Good luck,

Miriam

FROM NATALIE

Dear You,

I know all too well the feelings of utter hopelessness and self-hatred that accompany depression. I know what it is like to lie awake at night feeling like your head is going to explode because every worry you have ever had, every bad thing that has been said about you and everything you should have done is circling around and around relentlessly.

I know how it feels to live with a heart that is so heavy it almost suffocates you and eyes that refuse to cry. I know the feeling of pure desperation when you plead with the world to just give you a chance or a way through it, a magic pill or something. But with that said I also know what it feels like to break through the barbed wire that I had become entangled in, climb out of the dark hole I lived in that was filled with anger, bitterness and blame and I started to feel the warmth of the sun seep into my skin for the first time in a long time.

No matter how long you have been in that hole, how deep it is or how hopeless it seems to attempt to climb out of it, I am living, breathing proof that it is possible. There was no magic pill that I took that cured me from depression and anxiety although the correct medications do play a role in my recovery.

The catalyst for making the decision that depression would not rule me was the notion that I actually was good enough. I was worthy enough to live a happy, successful, fulfilling life. To me recovery is a daily thing, I have to keep working at it. I try to keep the philosophy that having one bad day does not mean I have a bad life. I learnt to appreciate the smaller things that I never noticed before and I taught myself that life is happier being an optimist than a pessimist. I realised that having a chemical imbalance that causes me to feel depressed does not actually mean anything about me, it is what it is and I can rise above.

I am no longer a scared, hopeless little girl who blames people for her misfortunes. I am a strong, independent, capable, beautiful person who just happens to have a mental illness. I made the choice to make the most of the cards I had been dealt and to try and use them in a way that could benefit myself and others.

I am learning to love myself for everything I am and everything that I am not. I am learning that it is okay to be different and I am learning to appreciate myself. I am learning to accept what I cannot change and instead to embrace it.

The first step towards recovery in my opinion is the decision to be in recovery. To value yourself and put a stop to self-destructive behaviour. Surrounding yourself with supportive and loving influences and removing the negative ones. Be kind to yourself, speak to yourself as you would to someone that you love and don't get discouraged by the bad times because they will come. If you need medication then that is okay and nothing to be ashamed of. Recovery is a fight for your own wellbeing and it is one that you can win.

I believe that you can do it because you are special and the world needs to know who you are.

Love,

Natalie

FROM PAUL

Dear You,

I know you can't concentrate for long at the moment and that your mind is elsewhere, so if you only remember one thing from this letter, make it this – the future is brighter than it looks.

How do I know this? Well, I have the luxury of writing this from nearly three years into your future. Trust me, it's a better place. Physically, it's the same place, so don't worry, there's no major upheaval. Mentally, though, it's a different world.

You know how you just don't look forward to anything at the moment? That will change.

You know those headaches you're getting every day? They won't last forever – nor will the blotchy skin or the other ailments.

You know those ferociously black moods and the bursts of anger and irritability that gnaw away at you? They will get fewer and farther between. And you know that complete lack of energy or enthusiasm? Fear not, you will get your mojo back. The insomnia will fade too.

So what advice can I give you? Quite a lot, when I think about it, but you have to be ready to take it so wait for a day when you are feeling more alert and receptive.

You've made the first step. You've realised you have a problem with stress and that you are completely frazzled. The doctor has told you that you have depression and has given you some medication.

So here is my first piece of advice. I know you want to get off that medication as quickly as possible, but don't set any targets and don't rush. I am still taking that medication and it doesn't bother me now. Okay, so no alcohol for three years doesn't sound great, but you can't hold your drink anyway, so it doesn't make much difference. When you're truly ready to come off the tablets, take your time and get it right.

Next, get yourself some counselling. The doctor can refer you. The tablets can manage your mood to some extent, but on their own they only deal with symptoms. You need to get to grips with what is causing your depression so that you can get better. It can be gruelling, but it is worth it.

You should also read a book called *Depressive Illness: The Curse of the Strong*, by Dr Tim Cantopher. He knows you can't concentrate for long and explains depression in a way you can understand in short bursts.

Two more things, then try and get some sleep, or maybe go out for some fresh air. Just try not to think too much, unless it's about things you enjoy doing. You need to do more of those things.

So, my final pearls of wisdom.

The road to recovery is long and bumpy. It goes up and down like a rollercoaster. But remember this – you are getting better. It's slow and it can feel like you are getting nowhere, but keep a diary of good things that happen, of positive feelings, of praise people give you, however small. On bad days, it will remind you that you are not a failure and that it's worth existing. Learn from it and believe it.

Finally, don't keep depression to yourself. It is not a dirty secret. The sooner you open up about it – maybe write a blog? – the sooner you'll find the many other people who have gone through the same thing or who are going through it right now.

I won't say, 'Chin up.' I certainly won't say, 'Man up.' All I will say is look after yourself and be as patient as you can.

You're worth it.

Paul

FROM BARBARA

Dear You,

I know how hard this is to hear, when hearing anything takes effort through a fog of indifference, but things will get better.

If your experience of depression is anything like mine, then right now, you are scared, at the bottom of a dark pit, with no way out. You can't do all this exercise they keep telling you will release endorphins and make you feel better, because getting up and dressed (on a good day) is enough to exhaust you let alone anything else. You can spend a whole day doing nothing, thinking of nothing.

People will ask you how you feel. What a ridiculous question. You feel nothing. If pushed you cry. A lot. Many things make you cry, and when you cry, you can't stop crying. What is the point of anything?

Does that sound familiar? Believe me, this is familiar to me – I've been there on and off my whole adult life.

Now just look up. Right up there, at the top of your deep, black pit, there's a glimpse of sunlight. That's your hope. And there are hands reaching down. Those are my hands, and the hands of everyone here who knows that level of despair. They are reaching to give you a touch, one human being to another, a touch that says, 'We're here. We have got better, we're up here in the daylight, and one day, you'll be back here too. And we're not going away. We won't abandon you. We understand.'

I don't know what your ladder out will be – friends, counselling, time, medication – I've done it lots of ways, but each time it does happen – hold on to that thought – It Does Happen – this time I got new medication. Horrible side-effects to start with, but now I'm stable and depression-free for a couple of years. That's amazing. That might not be your ladder, but there will be one. For now, just know it's there, and that we want to bring you comfort and hope. Someday you will reach for that first rung and you will be on your way to a brighter time.

I wish you well. I love your strength to make it through this. Have a big hug.

Barbara

FROM CHRISTINA

Dear You,

Although we have never met, in some respects, it is like looking in a mirror. I understand what it feels like to be in the dark depths of depression. I understand what it feels like to feel hopeless, like things will never be okay; that things will never get better. I understand what it feels like to think that your family would be better off if you were not even alive.

I am here today to share my story by the grace of God and because of my unbelievable support system. I am here today because I didn't remain silent. I spoke out about my feelings and my thoughts of harming myself. I am here today and I bring a message of hope and perseverance. I am here to tell you that things WILL get better. I promise you that and you have to believe it. Do not remain silent and alone in your illness.

I came from a very dark place. Every day was a struggle. It was a struggle to do the most simple tasks such as changing my clothes or taking a shower. I was afraid to care for my baby. I should have been a new mother full of joy and happiness and I wasn't. I was overwhelmed. I was full of anxiety over every little thing. I was deeply depressed.

My mother suffers from depression and bipolar disorder so I knew she would understand. I would often call her and tell her, 'I don't think I can do this any more. I am tired of fighting. I want to give up. My son deserves a normal mom.' She made me realise that I have to do this and I have to fight – for my son's sake – but more importantly for myself. I was worth it. My son needed ME. He needed me to be his mother. He would not be okay if I left him. I was the only person that could be that mom to him. No one else could fill that place in his life but me. That is what kept me going.

Climbing out of the depression happens in small steps, but each step is important and crucial to the healing process. Whether it is simply taking a shower, going for a walk, doing the dishes, or taking out the trash. It all makes a difference. Then all of a sudden one day you realise you are singing in the car to a song you like and you think – I am starting to feel better. There is another side – a better side – and you are well on the road to recovery.

It will happen for you. It will. You just have to hang in there and take it one step at a time. You will get there. Just give yourself that time to heal. Each day is a new day and each day brings a fresh start.

Here is hoping that today is the beginning of your fresh start. Take a deep breath and carry on. The people in your life need YOU and YOU are worth the fight.

Christina

FROM TALIA

Dear You,

I have been where you are. I know the despair that can take over every thought and drain the colour from a day. I remember how sadness can be overwhelming; that every step or bite or word can feel painful and raw and impossible. And for a little while, maybe it is not possible. It's okay if you can't do it today. It's not your fault; it's not something you can will away

I know that these moods can feel isolating and embarrassing. I understand how difficult it can be to be around people who cannot relate to what you are going through. If it helps, there are many out there who can, and those who can't may have the power to reach you from the other side. Let the people that love you throw you a life-rope, and though it may take time to grasp it, be comforted in the knowledge that it is there.

Remember the words of King Solomon: 'This too shall pass.'

It will help you remember that the bad times fade and that the good times are worth appreciating. I know that I will never 'lose' my depression. It comes and goes like an unruly houseguest in my brain. My approach is to find strategies to keep it at bay. Hold on to happy things and let go of things that threaten that happiness.

Run. Or walk. Or hula-hoop. I know it may take days or months to get the strength, but when you do, you will reap the benefits.

Be kind to yourself. Your body is the only place you will ever live and your mind is your key to unlocking the world. Although sometimes they may falter, they will never lose their value.

At times I have been tempted to romanticise my depression, pretending my tortured soul gives me a special status or insight into the world. The temptation to wallow in suffering is always there, but I have come to realise that simplicity and peace are far more attractive than tragedy and agony. Happiness is not a simple thing to achieve but there are small treasures within every part of life. Savour them.

You are not alone and your suffering does not lock you out of the rest of the world. Depression is a part of life, but remember the other things to live for that lie waiting for when the clouds pass.

Be kind to yourself. You may not be able to control how you feel, but you are strong for experiencing it and persevering.

Don't forget the dreams of your childhood self: to be happy and healthy, and explore the world.

When you feel better, you will.

Good luck, and my thoughts are with you.

Talia

An illness that takes away hope and joy is the cruellest of all, so getting through the day makes you the strongest of all.

FROM MICHAEL

Dear You,

In the not-too-distant past, I was one of those people that believed that there is no such thing as depression. That everyone gets sad. That it was a cop-out. A sign of weakness, by those who can't cope.

I was wrong. As I experienced, it's real. Very real.

Over a period of months, I became absolutely paralysed. Every day was too much. Everything shut down.

I couldn't write. And I couldn't think, except for the cycling fears and the anxieties. I wouldn't interact with those around me. I didn't want to be around any more.

And as I think about it today, 'battle' may be the wrong word. Because I'm not sure it's something you win or lose.

But, on the other hand, maybe 'battle' is precisely the right word.

Maybe surviving is winning.

Maybe being able to share this story with others, and even with myself, is winning.

Because I did survive.

Though I didn't see how, I did reach somewhere deep inside and returned from that deep darkness, that place of self-hatred where everything seemed pointless. And somewhere on that journey, I've learned that depression is part of me.

Others, like author Dr Andrew Solomon, have gone even further. He has found a way to go beyond acceptance and to see beauty in his depression:

> I think that while I hated being depressed and would hate to be depressed again, I've found a way to love my depression. I love it because it has forced me to find and cling to joy. I love it because each day I decide, sometimes gamely, and sometimes against the moment's reason, to cleave to the reasons for living. And that, I think, is a highly privileged rapture.

'To love my depression.' Wow. I can't say that I see it that way, as much as I'd like to say that I do. I don't love it. I don't even like it. But I have accepted it. And through this, I have learned more about who I am. I know myself more deeply, and I recognise that I have light and also darkness. And that they fit together in some weird way.

I am richly complicated. We all are. And this makes me feel more whole.

Though I hope to never go through another episode, having been through this, in a strange way, also makes me feel more alive. It has forced me to be more in touch with my emotions. I feel like I've grown, like my focus on what's important and what matters to me is sharper. I have also learned through this that the best thing we can do is to be open about it and be kind to each other. To watch our friends and our loved ones. To support each other. To be patiently loving. At first glance this may sound like a platitude, like some Pollyanna, kumbaya notion. It's not. Depression or not, that's truly what it's all about.

I can't tell you how many people I have been open with these past years about my depression only to find out that they too have been through it or are struggling with it. They are empathetic and caring, because they know what it's like.

And it's not only others suffering from depression, but friends who simply understand the need for patience, kindness and love. Who know they can't just tell you to 'get happy', 'enjoy life' or 'snap out of it'. Who stick with you, who reach out persistently, even when you seem to fade away.

That has been incredibly soothing. It has let me know that I'm not alone, that others have been through this same thing, felt these same feelings.

This experience has also made me more sensitive and aware of the pain we all carry.

Everyone. We all carry pain. We all carry sadness. We all get confused. We all struggle.

Being sensitive to the pain and needs of others makes me feel more human. It makes me feel more connected to the world; not less.

When you think about it, that's really incredible. Because that feeling of connection, it's the exact opposite of loneliness.

That this feeling can spring from the ultimate loneliness and pain of depression is hopeful, invigorating and impossibly delicious. Never forget that.

Michael

FROM JEMMA

Dear You,

I'm not going to ask how you are. I remember that feeling too well. See, 18 months ago I was you. I remember so well the torment and torrent of feelings. But that's all it is now, a memory. I know, I wouldn't believe me either.

It's hard to believe and imagine a time beyond this pain. But I promise you, it is there. Waiting for you, when you're ready. It's not impatient. Just...waiting. And no matter how long you take to get there, it will just sit there: waiting patiently for you to be ready to embrace it.

Just take a deep breath. Go on. And another. Every breath is you still living. And even if that's all you manage today, I remember what an achievement that is on the bad days. You're achieving something with every breath you take.

And I'm proud of you.

Jemma

FROM HANNE

Dear You,

Depression sucks, you know? Well, you probably know. I do, too.

For me it all started six years ago, and it went hand in hand with restrictive eating that soon spiralled out of control into a full-blown eating disorder.

In fact, if all those years ago people would have told me that everything would get better, I would have merely nodded my head while screaming my disbelief on the inside. I thought things simply couldn't improve, that I'd be forever trapped in the dark room I felt myself imprisoned in. I felt locked in, unable to fight my way back to the surface.

While my friends went out, I chose to remain home. When I attended parties, I could not help but think I'd have had a better time on my own. Even when I was surrounded by others, I felt like a bubble shut me out, like I was somehow different from the others. And even when I found myself in the intensive care department of the hospital, I still could not bring myself to reclaim my life.

At the time, my path to self-destruction seemed so easy. That is, until I opened my eyes and came to realise how much pain I was putting my family through. With every lash I took at myself, I was lashing out at them too. Fighting for perfection, I damaged them as much as I damaged myself. That's when I knew I needed to change. That's when I realised my struggle for control made me all the more powerless. I needed to take over the reins of my life.

And I did. I found new ways to get my troubles off my chest. Ones that didn't involve food or restriction; ones that didn't leave the pain cooped up inside.

I began to write. I published a novel, inspired and motivated others with it. I started a YouTube channel, read books and worked on creative art projects. I kept a diary and still do to this day.

I am not always happy with my life, my body and my achievements. But that is okay. You don't need perfect happiness to live a fulfilling life. What you do need, however, is to learn to accept yourself and be okay with yourself. What you do need is to see how far you have come, and what you have achieved. You don't need to love your life in order to accept it, and that is the first step in recovery.

So go and get lost in your hobbies. Go and learn to love yourself again. Keep fighting.

You, too, can get through this.

Hanne Arts

FROM HARRIET

Dear You,

I understand how bleak you feel, really, I do.

You see, I've been there too. I've been stuck in a helpless bleak limbo, so dark and frightening. My words failed me, my laugh was but a distant memory that I thought would never return. Tears would flow uncontrollably until they dried up and even opening my eyes was an effort.

The thought of ever getting better was beyond me, but I did, I recovered and I began to laugh again. It was like all my Christmases had come at once. It was a miracle, I thought.

You too will get better, I promise.

Be patient my friend and be kind to yourself in the meantime.

Harriet

FROM PETER

Dear You,

I know the very place you are at; I have been to this exact
same place, and sat where you are right now. Looked out,
only to feel a total all-encompassing black lifeless void
where I thought I'd previously existed. I've been there
on and off for periods of my life — sometimes weeks,
sometimes months. It knows me, I know it.

There is, and can only be, one place so bleak and so
empty as this. Only one place that could be so absolutely
and unequivocally...well...nothing. And when I'm there
(where you are now) everything is so very 'clear' to
me: that life is completely pointless, that I am a total
failure, that love is always fake or fatally flawed, that
we are all just flesh and no soul. The love I felt for
my beautiful children, my friends and my family, the
promise of a new day, or anything of previous beauty
and unquestionable meaning; all lost power over
me now.

And yet, how strange it was. Despite all of this
emptiness, I could still sit and feel my soft beating

heart and the living breathing frame that made me what I thought I was. But the flesh made no response in defence at this all-out assault at its very core. Only sat in idle function, passive, disconnected, empty and abandoned. More of a living death walled around a living body.

'How do you feel today, Peter?' It struck me there was simply no answer to that from where I was sat in the doctor's chair – you would need access to some basic level of human feelings to give any kind of response. Because you don't feel anything – nothing, just nothing at all. To even ask such a question meant they didn't even know where I was. This place, so real and so cruel to us, is cruelly invisible to those that want to help us the most.

Then, just when I saw no hope, no salvation, I thought I cannot take this any more, that, if it was actually humanly possible to die of hopelessness alone, it would be this way now. But one day, a moment, a touch, a kind of sunrise, a chink of a sense of life and of living that was mine to grasp came through.

So my hands reached out; I lifted myself up; reached out. Swam up like breaking the surface of a bottomless lifeless ocean, gasping for breath, feeling alive again from when I was sure I had long since been crushed and drowned. And so the hope returned. The life, the love, I could now begin to see and feel again from within my senses. My heart, mine own once more, cradled my soul like a mother's arms.

Why did this fool doubt how beautiful I am? How wonderful his love is? How beautiful nature really is? How could he not see how much he loves those he holds so dear to him and without whom life really would be without meaning?

I actually pity those who haven't been to where you are now; where we both go to, sometimes. Who can really appreciate or know the true value of their life, more than those who lose it all, then find it again? You will too.

Peter

FROM NATASHA

Dear You,

I'm extremely sorry that you're feeling this way right now. It isn't fair and it isn't right – mental illness never is. But I, a chronically depressed, treatment-resistant person, am here to tell you that there is another side to the pain. I know it feels like there isn't, but I promise, there is.

When depression lays its heavy, spikey, leaden blanket on you, I know it feels like everything is impossible. I know it feels like you're buried six feet under in muck and slime. I know sometimes you don't shower for weeks. I know it's tempting not to change your clothes for days and days. I know you don't want to cook yourself any real food for a month.

I know what it feels like when every cell in your body hurts. I know what it feels like to seem to fail at everything you do. I know what it's like to take medication that seems to only produce side-effects and never makes you feel better. I know what it's like not to love yourself and I know what it's like to think that death is the only way out of the pain.

Because of this, your life may have fallen apart around you. It may feel like you can't do a thing about it. It can feel like reaching out to fix it is like trying to catch water with an open hand. I know that all of this hurts immensely.

But here's the thing: I also know what it feels like to start lifting your way out of that dreck. I also know what it feels like to take a baby step forward. I know what it feels like to get up, and make yourself a grilled tomato and cheese sandwich after only eating ice cream for days. I also know what it feels like to take a deep breath and to have it relieve some of the pain that you've been feeling.

I know what the road to recovery feels like.

This road is a long and bumpy one – there are switchbacks and mountainous hills and treacherous turns; but this road truly does exist and you can find it. You can navigate it. It's not easy. You'll have to take it one tiny step at a time, but you can do it.

Keep working with your psychiatrist. Keep talking to your therapist. Continue using your coping skills. Follow your treatment plan. Maintain your healthy life-style changes. These are things that can help you find the roadmap to recovery. I know, sometimes, it feels like no matter what you do, it doesn't help. But these things do help – over time. I know that waiting for them to work is agony. But it is an agony you can survive in order to live a good life again.

Because in the end, what you will experience on the other side of the pain will make slogging through it worth it. I have experienced skydives and flying with eagles over the mountains of Venezuela and starting a major mental health blog at NatashaTracy.com and falling in love – all post-depression. And there is nothing special about me. If I can survive it, so can you. What you need to know is that another side exists and you can get there. I'm not saying it's easy but I am saying it's possible.

You can do it.

Natasha

FROM ALAN

Dear You,

My friend, please allow me the privilege of calling you this as I hope by the end of this, you will sense that is what I am and open to be there for you if you need one. An ear to listen, a voice to calm your fears, a smile to reassure that you're not alone.

Some call our illness the disease of loneliness. Our illness is invisible and we can and do feel so isolated as to be socially invisible to those around us. Even those that care cannot see the heart-crushing pain that you feel right now; the feeling that you can't go through another of those terrible times. The interminable confusion in your mind, the inability to concentrate, the lack of energy just to lift the weight of the duvet and face the day or, worse, to fight it any longer.

Though I know you may not see or know this yet if you're still in the depths of the hole where you can see nothing but blackness all around you, there are people who care. I am one who has seen its universal bleakness and experienced the bleaker reality of suffering without the cushion of love; but that began to end when I started to reach out and talk. And I was surprised by what I heard from those around me, how many had their own similar experiences or just how many cared. Of course there is ignorance too but that is the exception and not the norm. I am one who sees and hears you. And I care. That's why I write this openly to you.

Every day is still a challenge for me and it will probably remain so for some time to come. But that's okay. Yes that's right, it's okay. It's okay to accept this because that means we have the strength to take this on – challenge its humbling lows and excruciating pain. I don't always have my shit together – I still have incredibly bad days, if you wonder how I can write this now when you feel you couldn't possibly, don't, because like you a few months ago I could not read more than two words of one line of a single paragraph that you have read so far.

You currently live in a world that is irrevocably disordered and chaotic. Don't think or wish that you have to totally control the chaos inside your head, keep it inside and not let it out, make perfect choices, be perfect at work. I tried that, it did not work. It could not work. At times you may feel that the illness is spoiling your life and those you love, that everyone could be better off without you. But many will owe the happiness of their life to you. It's sometimes just difficult to see that.

For now, try not to struggle on; know you can ask for help and people will be there for you. Know that I for one will respect you whatever you do. Whatever you feel. Whatever you choose. Also know that you are not alone and never will be.

Your friend,

Alan

FROM SARA

Dear You,

If you're reading this, then you're probably having a bad day, or even a bad week or two; it happens from time to time.

What I'm going to tell you, you may not believe, but it's true: It won't last forever.

You may be sat there reading this, thinking that there's no hope or happiness to be found; doubting yourself, your strength, who you are as a person even; you may even have that annoying poison parrot sitting on your shoulder, whispering sweet nothings of negativity constantly; and you may even be planning your way out. DON'T.

There will be better days, maybe even tomorrow. I hope you're listening to me now, because here are the most important things to remember:

You ARE strong.

You ARE capable.

You CAN get through this.

You WILL beat the black dog.

I know that it doesn't feel like it right now, and everything is really overwhelming and scary. I know that the intrusive thoughts are screaming and won't give you a break for even five minutes. I know that all you want to do is cry, hide away or even end it all.

You have people that love, care and want to support you. Turn to them for help, don't battle this alone. Shutting yourself away is the worst thing you can do. Ask for help, and I'm sure they'll be there for you.

Look at how far you've come; you have fought through tougher times and came out victorious on the other side. Yes, today may well be a bad day, but it's not infinite.

Soon you'll reach the end and step on the bottom of a ladder. Keep searching for that ladder. It IS there, and you WILL find it and come back up again. Trust me. Never give up HOPE that better days are just around the corner, all you've got to do is tough it out for today, scratch it up to experience and move on.

You made it through yesterday, and you can make it through today, tomorrow and beyond.

You are STRONGER than you believe you are.

Remember this mantra: REFUSE TO SINK, INSTEAD LEARN TO FLY.

Find your wings and soar up, up and away from all the negativity. You know you can do it.

You're a WARRIOR.

You're a SURVIVOR.

You know that inside of you there is a fire burning, fan the flames and get that head up. How can you see where you're going if you keep looking at your feet? Look forward, not down or back.

There are better days ahead, and one day, you'll read this and think, 'Hey, she was right! Look at me now, I'm doing great!'

So now then little fighter, chin up and show the world that smile, things will get brighter.

You got this.

Love, Sara x

FROM IZZY

Dear You,

I remember. That sinking sick feeling, the loss of control, watching everything slip away, feeling paralysed. Feeling as if you are just existing and there is no way to live.

This is how I felt on and off for years. Depression for me gradually got worse and worse, like a parasite. BUT once it had got way past feeling worse than any feeling I had ever experienced, slowly gradually, as it had got worse, it very gradually got better. I took baby steps. At first, getting out of bed was an accomplishment. The next day, getting dressed was. The day after I was unable to move again. But the day after that I was able to get up and get dressed.

After tons of meds, hospitalisations, psychosis, believing that no one was in my exact situation so they couldn't know that I would get better...I got better.

I still struggle some days of course. But the darkness has lifted.

I am able to live again.

And what was my biggest healer personally? Time. Time made me so ill but time also got me through. Meds helped, CBT helped, a friend helped, music helped. Time healed.

In darkness, the sun will rise again. Always.

Love from Izzy xxx

FROM NATALIE

Dear You,

Sitting in Accident & Emergency, sobbing inconsolably, being told things would get better seemed like a fantasy. I was convinced that I no longer wanted to be here. I could not take life any more and was no longer prepared to suffer. Medication and counselling had not fixed me. I had nothing...or so I thought. I was constantly told that things would eventually feel different, by numerous health professionals and the few friends I had let in. How could they know? They were not going through this! They had not experienced what I had, to get to this point, abuse, neglect, stress...there was no hope. I did not believe them.

I do now because I am better. I am not suffering from suicidal thoughts constantly. I do believe that I can have a good life. I know life will not be easy all the time, but I am more prepared to deal with it. I am being proactive and going on courses about depression, having counselling, taking care of myself and have a new job. I used to think it was selfish to care about me but it is a necessity. You cannot do anything for anyone until the healing starts.

I cannot wait for you to see how life is, free of depression. It is amazing. You look forward to waking up each day. To going outside and smiling because the sky is blue and the sun is shining, feeling the warm sun on your skin. It feels like the sun has been missing for a long time. Then you notice that your smile has made someone else smile. You realise that you would not have been able to experience these things if you were no longer alive. You look forward to seeing friends, who you can genuinely laugh with again. You might have a bad day but the good days outweigh them. You can finally experience what you have been missing out on. I cannot wait to welcome you to the survivors gang. There are lots of us. We have been to that dark place but have come back up, and found the light.

You will too.

The time that you felt so bad feels so long ago, as if it were a dream. You tell yourself every day that your past won't steal your future. Your future is now yours to make of it what you will.

Natalie Louise

Things that weaken depression:

talking about it,

not doing what it tells you,

not believing it.

FROM NATASCHA

Dear You (and Me),

This letter is about nothing and everything. My life is perfect. Supportive family, wonderful husband, hilarious son. I'm a doctor and I love my job. But sometimes, I'm not well. It's not the overwhelming gut-wrenching sadness that's the worst, that's when I know I'm not very well. Throat-constricting sobbing and quiet screaming – that's all feelings.

It's when the nothing arrives. I stupidly think, 'Oh finally, some relief.'

But then

nothing,

nothing,

nothing.

It can be hours, days or weeks but it always seems like forever.

Just nothing.

I have nothing to say to my wonderful husband, nothing to add at my dream job. I stop answering the phone to my supportive and hilarious friends and family. Just nothing. Colours are more grey, music is only noise and the perfect life is in a perfect bubble, and I can't reach it. I can't ever see the end or the light or even know if it's coming. But it does. It always does. A little at first, like a firefly. A little shimmer over water. Then the spell is broken. Like the banks of the river bursting, life is back. I can feel. I'm back in the bubble. I cherish my time there because it is marvellous. I know one day nothing might come back. I have to remind myself it always goes away, and that is everything.

That's why this letter is to You and Me.

Best Wishes,

Natascha

FROM TIM

Dear You,

This is not how it has to be, this is not how it will always be, you can and will get better. I know, I am surviving it.

I know how it feels to think all is hopeless, to think there is nothing valuable or worthy about myself, that all the people close to me who assure me there is good in me don't really know me and would recoil if they could really *see* me for what I am. I know how it is to be tired of the exhausting, draining, lack of any enjoyment, the drab colourless existence. At times I wished I had the energy or the courage to end it all. At times, what stopped me was the stigma my family would have to live with after a suicide. I did not even believe it would actually matter if I died. I did not believe I was important enough or worth it. I was not worried about causing them great pain, as I did not even believe there would be any.

Those feelings and thoughts are not really you, they are the illness. And you are not weak, it is not your fault, it is an illness that does not respect age, sex, background, status, or anything else. And there is treatment for it. Please, talk to your doctor; if he is not sympathetic, talk to someone: a friend, a relative, a Samaritan, anyone. There is help, and you will get better.

There is colour in life, it does get better. I sought help three years ago, and am on the way to recovery. It is worth getting out of bed in the morning. I am starting to live again, not just survive, and not just exist. Life is still hard, but it is worth the struggle again for me, and it will be for you.

You are unique, and you are worthwhile. This world is made up of billions of fallible, beautiful human beings like you and me. Hang in there, it IS worth it. Please, hang in there.

With all the love and hope I can give you,

Tim

FROM Q. S. LAM

Dear You,

I write this letter in the early hours of the morning thinking if my words help one person then that is something.

Often I wish I could exchange my mind for another one, a spotless one that is steeped in eternal sunshine, instead of the dented one that feels chronically polluted. But this is the mind that I have and I know that there is good within it, in the paintings that I create, the poems that bubble and grow out of the mouldy debris.

To dispel the blocks of mental rubbish that clog up my brain I have started a happy book, which is small and easy to carry. It contains drawings and paintings and upon each new page I date it and write my achievements of the day, such as 'read book to my child', 'watered the plants', 'worked on painting', 'went to the post office', and these little moments build up to create a picture of my day that is contrary to the one in my head.

These small moments help to remind me of who I am and where I am going and what I hope to achieve and do, they keep me anchored to the present. Sometimes I can forget to write it in my 'happy book', or misplace it, but if that is the case you can create a 'mental' happy book and remind yourself of these small achievements, which can help to dispel the erroneous negative narratives we can often get ensnared in. There are other things you can do such as try to divert your mind through reading, breathing, writing, drawing, singing or simply talking to a friend over a cup of tea and a slice of cake   all of these things can have a palliative impact on a tired, battered brain. Kindness is key, there is a tendency to beat ourselves with a big stick, it's a bad habit, we have to try to stop it, since no one deserves such incessant internal abuse. We have to find a way to silence that cruel voice and befriend it instead and no longer be afraid of it either.

The mind can become a suffocating prison without a 'tent of blue' to peer out of, I try to unlock the door and walk out of that prison towards the meadows, towards the light, and lie down in the grass, look up at the sky, see the shapes in the clouds or the patterns in the stars, watch the birds as they fly and dream that life can get better, if I let it. Indeed, it can, if only a tiny bit – a tiny bit is something to cherish.

Please don't feel stuck in the darkness, I know what it's like; you are not alone. May your life get that little bit brighter, I believe that it can and it will.

You have to look at each day like a new canvas and decide the painting you want your day to be rather than paint the same old dark picture that just compounds that sense of doom, gloom and hopelessness. You have to choose the colours you want your painting to be even if your default stance is to go for morose shades of grey and black. There are flecks of light and colour in each day, tiny ones like a bright ochre, or a vivid scarlet. These iridescent colours shine and smile out at us all. They are friendly and warm. These colours can guide you towards a brighter place and help you paint a different sort of painting. A painting that when you look at it speaks to you like an old friend, inspires, comforts and stirs something deep inside, you just have to open your eyes a little wider and let those colours in.

Take good care of yourself, be kind to yourself, be your number one ally, and keep searching for that fleck of light sleeping in the shadows. It is there, I can see that tiny fleck right now – put it in your pocket and cherish it.

From,

Q. S. Lam

FROM LISA

Dear You,

Thank you for opening this letter. You probably won't be reading much at the moment. So I need to grab your attention.

I want to tell you something. I have been where you are, or my own version of it. Depression (or whatever you prefer to call how you are feeling at the moment) is different for each of us. And there are different sorts. But that really doesn't matter. What makes you and me similar is the utter awfulness of our experience. The weariness, even exhaustion, and yet inability to sleep. Lying awake for hour after endless hour, either alone or next to a partner who you can't talk to about the darkness of your thoughts. How pointless everything seems, especially in the mornings. How things you used to look forward to feel trivial and too much effort. How worried you are about stuff you used not to worry about, and even more worried over things that were worrying you already. And how loathsome and undeserving you feel, in every possible way.

Let me tell you a secret. When I was last ill, not all that long ago, I wanted to be dead. I even felt jealous of people with terminal illnesses like cancer because they had a reason for staying in bed and dying and people wouldn't think badly of them for it. And yet at the same time, I didn't actually believe I was ill. I went along with my psychiatrist and GP because I thought I must, and I didn't have the energy to argue with them. But inside, I knew I was a lazy, work-shy, cowardly, incompetent, self-obsessed waste of space.

Now let's talk about you. You are a wonderful person, with many fabulous and interesting things that make you who you are. It is just that you have lost sight of these for a little while. I've been visited by depression many times, each different in its own vile way. From my experience, and that of many others who have generously shared theirs, the special things that make you who you are will come back. It is just that the strength, patience and hope you need to wait for them to return is exactly what depression takes away. So right now, everything feels impossible. I truly know that feeling.

Depression is an illness. It can actually be seen in the brain. It may get better on its own. But depending on how severe it is, that can take ages. However bad things seem right now, if you don't seek help, they could get worse. You may have already found that it helps to talk to a friend, or call a helpline. If not, however hard it feels, please think hard about giving this a try.

Your doctor can help you. He/she can support you to decide if you need medication and/or a talking therapy, or a referral to more specialist services. If you are prescribed them, the new antidepressant medications work with your body to help you heal. Yes, they do have side-effects. But so do antibiotics and you would probably take those if you had a serious infection. People and websites that tell you that taking antidepressants is a sign of weakness honestly don't know what they are talking about. Please don't take advice from anyone who isn't a qualified doctor. If you are prescribed medication, I hope you will consider taking it, including waiting for it to start working, which can take a few weeks, and avoiding the things you should avoid while you are on it. And if you are referred for a talking therapy, or a group, please give yourself a chance, however anxious or low you are, and give serious consideration to going along.

Some of us find sharing what we perceive as our 'weaknesses' very hard. I know I do. But bottling things up is not a good idea. My biggest breakthrough has been learning to share how I feel with those close to me. I have to keep practising. And so will you. It is very hard, but worth the effort.

I could write pages and pages about how you WILL get better. But your concentration is probably not great right now. And there are other lovely letters here that I hope you will also read.

I just want to end with this. You will have good days and bad days. In time, you will gradually notice that there are more good ones than bad ones. You will rejoice again in small things, like a walk in the rain, or the smile of a stranger. You will find things to do that give you a sense of achievement. I did jigsaw puzzles and very bad knitting. You can choose your own. Just make the tasks small and achievable. And celebrate what you have done. Because you are amazing to have found the strength to do them.

Learning to be kind to yourself can be a lifelong project. But if you aren't kind to yourself, it is much harder to be kind to other people. So for that reason, it is a generous and thoughtful thing to do, rather than an indulgence, as you may once have thought it.

Thank you for reading this. And well done. It was a huge step.

I wish you luck on the rest of your journey. And please know this: you are not alone.

With my loving kindness for your gradual recovery.

Lisa

FROM AL

Dear You,

In my case, depression seemed to come out of nowhere. I remember dropping off a good friend and saying to him, 'Something is going on. I just don't feel like myself.' From that point on, things went downhill. I wasn't communicating well with people, I was struggling to get sleep due to my racing mind, and I could barely eat. Any time I was out with my wife, when we returned home, I'd ask her if I'd done alright (socially). I began to take medicine and see a therapist. Things continued to deteriorate. I would somehow manage to mask my depression at work, hold it together fairly well with my kids when I returned home and eventually break down and have uncontrollable crying bouts in the evening.

I went back to the psychiatrist to inform him of my suicidal thoughts. He increased the medication. My crying bouts increased and my suicidal thoughts became more detailed and pervasive, occurring throughout the day and even in a dream. I brought my wife and sister to the next psychiatrist appointment so that they could help communicate just how bad things had gotten and advocate for more support. I made the decision to take three weeks off work and checked myself into a partial hospitalisation programme.

Please know that you will get better. I did and many, many others have. It takes work and effort. I would urge you to consider multiple strategies to work towards recovery, rather than relying on just one. Here are some suggestions I have for you to consider:

- Contact one or two close friends and share with them what is going on. Ask for their support. This may just be requesting that they send you a hopeful text a couple of times a week or invite you out for breakfast or a coffee.
- Reach out to family members (your parents, siblings, cousins, aunts and uncles, significant others, etc.). Have trust that they care about you and your situation.
- Join a support group. The more narrow focus, the better. While others may not be able to really understand what you're going through and how it feels, these people will. This is a great way to receive support and to support others once you are feeling better. It's instantly a group of trusted individuals who have been through similar challenges. I still attend a men's depression support group twice a month.
- Try to exercise, even if it means a short walk around the block in the beginning. Little by little increase the amount of time you're exercising and/ or the rigour.

- Consider journalling. I journalled every night while going through my depression. At the end of every entry, I included a piece in which I wrote, 'Today, in order to work towards my recovery, I...' Sometimes it may have been a list of something quite simple such as, 'I drove my kids to school.' This is one way of recognising your small successes!
- Consider medication and talk therapy. If you are trying talk therapy for the first time, do not give up on it if you don't like your therapist. You may need to shop around a bit, unfortunately, in order to find a therapist with whom you really click.
- Try to get back into an old hobby or start a new one. While I was in the partial hospitalisation programme, I began to make pictures with pastels. I continue this new hobby and share it with my children. I also started to play the guitar.

These are just a few ideas to help you begin to move in the right direction. I believe the more strategies you utilise, the quicker the recovery. It's critical that you seek out help. Too many people mask their depression and many begin to self-medicate. Reach out for the help that you need. Accept the help. Make the effort necessary to recover. I know this is easier said than done, I've been there.

Small steps. You will get there. You will recover. You are not alone!

With compassion,

Al

FROM CEINWEN

Dear You,

If you are reading this you must be struggling, finding it hard to find anything in your life of any worth. It is not that long ago I too felt that way.

Maybe all you can do is wish you could end your endless suffering. Life has become an existence, just wanting to sleep to escape from the endless thoughts of your worthlessness. You may have lost all hope and cannot see any possibility of your life improving. Full of guilt and shame, did you draw the curtains today or even this week, or month? Did you get washed or dressed? Is the place such a mess all you can do is run back to bed and hide under the duvet?

That was me; behind closed curtains I spent months in a state of unclean shame. Wishing I could end it all, take every pill in the house, but knowing failure would be even worse, and success cause pain for the few that still cared.

They said I had felt this way before and got over it, but they were wrong, I'd never lost all hope, all motivation before. 'You have to try,' they said, not understanding I had tried all year, and this was the result. A whole year I strived to forge a network of people and activities, things to make my life worthwhile. I opened doors only to find there was nothing inside for me. Spent time in rooms but was pushed outside. Confusion, anxiety and panic finally took over. It is with gratitude I thank those who with their gentle words and gift of time made sure I was safe at these times.

Maybe I had tried too hard but the alternative was total isolation. Now, with nothing left to try with, I could take no more, so I retreated. I hid from the world I did not belong in, and could not cope with, every simple task was impossible. I grappled with what had happened, asked myself what I had done that was so wrong. This was how it was and how it would be forever.

Hello you, are you still reading? Does any of the above resonate with you? Is there no pleasure in your life and your head full of horrible thoughts, all hope and optimism long gone? If so please keep reading because your life can improve, just like mine has.

Medication helped to ease the anxiety and panic but the depression and worthlessness still held a firm grip on me. It took time and a lot of patience from a couple of friends who always texted, phoned and visited me. They never judged me, always recognised and praised any small achievements like getting dressed or drawing the curtains. Eventually I was able see that they visited because they liked me and cared for me, and though I still felt unworthy it gave me some comfort and protection.

I was lucky with the mental health team who offered me a support worker. I'd never had a support worker before and did not know what to expect. What I got was someone that listened and understood. Together we shared many coffees and went shopping. I was reintroduced to my creative side when she took me to a local group where I weaved, sewed, made papier mâché, but more importantly connected with people. My desire to be close to nature was rekindled – watching it, shaping it – and I returned to maintaining a women's centre garden as a volunteer, raking up all the leaves and planting bulbs.

If anyone had told me I would be writing this in those dark days last year I would not have believed them. Put simply, the impossible became possible.

I'm still scared, but I'm walking again and I'm enjoying finding where this walk goes.

I hope soon you too will be able to take those first steps and find a walk that is enjoyable and a life that has meaning and above all HOPE.

Ceinwen

FROM KENNEDY

Dear You,

I understand that you don't want to get out of bed today.
You don't want to talk to anyone about anything. You just
feel as if living is a waste of time.

I'm here to tell you recovery is possible. Pain is
temporary and you can overcome anything.

Some day your cloudy skies will turn blue and the sun
will shine down and show you all of your beauty that
you can't see now.

Just never give up, I didn't, and I don't want you to either.

Remember, scars are a sign you are strong, not weak.

Love,

Kennedy

FROM JOHN

....

Dear You,

My name is John and I suffer from depressive episodes. They began in my early teens and continued, untreated, until I was 51. I'm now 53 and have been in treatment for two years. I believe that I'll remain in treatment for many years to come, and that's okay. It took many years to get as ill as I became, so it's no surprise to me that it'll take many years to heal.

In the beginning, the depressive episodes were fleeting, a mere day-long visit of a bleak mood. Over the years, the depth of bleakness and its duration both grew in intensity. By the time I was 51 the episode I was experiencing had lasted years and was very bleak.

I could go on and describe the worthlessness I felt, the fatigue, the weight of the depressive episode and more. You already know this from your own experience. Know then that while I can't know your pain, it's unique to you, I can certainly understand.

I begin by making a confession. On 2 September 2014, when I was 51, I attempted to take my own life. I make this confession to you so that you know just how distraught I was, how lacking in self-worth I was.

On 3 September, I was a very different person than just the day before. I was still broken, but I'd realised that I needed to find out what was wrong. If you're reading this letter, you've come to that same realisation and for that I commend you.

My recovery has been slow yet steady. It has, to be honest, been anything but linear. It's been filled with ups and downs, steps forward and steps back and the occasional wrong turn. Nonetheless, I'm now in a much better place.

My recovery began when I asked for help. That's all it took, that simple request. But it was a request that was beyond my ability to voice for far too long. For too long I was ashamed of myself, but you already know that feeling, and that shame kept me silent.

Once I found that voice, that inner strength to seek help, things changed for the better. I learned that I was ill, that my illness had a name and that it also had known methods of treatment. Naming it took away much of the power of the darkness I'd lived in for so long. Naming it revealed its weaknesses.

For example, major depressive disorder, the name, tries to instil a pervasive feeling of unworthiness, the lie. It places a filter on our thoughts and emotions where rational thought is unwelcome and emotion is incomplete. The emotion that we experience leaves out all the positives that exist around us. You know what I mean, that world that you see where people laugh and love and find enjoyment that's just that little bit beyond your reach.

The filter of major depressive disorder lies to us. It's the action of this filter that tells us we are poor at this and poor at that, while the reality is that we are no worse nor no better than everyone else. We are, as you know yourself, ill. Once you see this filter for the manipulative tool it is, you can begin to see through its deceit. And recovery can happen.

The first success in my recovery was to ask my parents for help. The second was to make a simple phone call, connect with the Canadian Mental Health Agency, and again ask for help. To my continuing good fortune, they listened and accepted my request, although, like any bureaucracy, it wasn't immediate. I mention this so you won't be surprised at the inevitable delays in treatment that you'll face.

Such simple acts: a decision to seek help and a phone call to initiate it. These acts are within your ability. They're no harder than your effort to get out of bed, and I know you can do that, on some days. So on one of those better days, and they do come, I encourage you to make this same phone call to the mental health agency in your area.

In this I'll bring to you attention 'The Four Agreements' of Don Miguel Ruiz and especially the fourth agreement which is to Always Do Your Best. On 3 September, my best, all I was able to do, was ask for help. No more, no less. On 4 September, my best was to locate a telephone number and call it. On some days, my best was to stay in bed. But each day I did my best, whatever that best may have been. And in so doing I propelled my recovery. I've no doubt that you can do this as well.

Remember when I mentioned that major depressive disorder is deceitful? You can challenge that deceit by keeping a list of your successes. Each day, write what you accomplished that day, write what your best was. Your illness will tell you that there was none, but your own words will show the truth and break through the deceit. Once again, this is such a simple thing to do, a simple thing within your capabilities.

My final request of you: please maintain a Gratitude Journal. Each night, before you go to bed, write down what you are grateful for that day. Contemplate upon it, allowing the feeling of gratitude to fill you. If you can, write three things. If you cannot, write the same thing three times. Maintain that feeling of gratitude as you slip away into sleep. As with everything else I ask of you, I know this to be within your abilities. I know this, because it was within mine. I can't express to you how very beneficial maintaining a Gratitude Journal has been to me, but I do know that I began to look forward to the coming morning and saw it for the opportunity it truly was.

I must close now. After reading this you are undoubtedly tired and overwhelmed. I know I am from writing it.

I wish you well and success in your journey.

Your friend,

John

FROM JOSEPH

Dear You,

I have suffered from a reactive depression for much of my adult life; marital breakdown, coming to terms with my sexuality and guilt at the break-up of my family being the primary causes.

Coming from a Roman Catholic background I was very familiar with the adage that 'God helps those who help themselves.' This became my mantra; I put all my energies into my work as a mental health professional and blocked out the black thoughts. This worked for a while, and then all of a sudden without warning I was a wreck. In retrospect all the signs were there but I was so focused on helping myself that I had forgotten what an insidious beast depression can be.

For the first time in my life I experienced the awesome power of the mind. At times I was overwhelmed by the strength of the feelings of complete worthlessness coupled with suicidal ideation, and yet conversely at other times I felt that I existed in a void with no emotions whatsoever. I was fortunate that my GP was sufficiently aware of mental health issues that she recognised that I was not ready for 'talking therapies' at that stage, and that I needed medication in order to lift my mood to allow me to engage.

I was aware that medication could take up to six weeks to really take effect; six minutes felt too long to continue in this state, I needed to feel better immediately. Two trips to A&E one week apart had very different outcomes. The first time I was petrified that the duty psychiatrist was going to detain me, on the second occasion I was terrified of being sent home. Psychiatric wards are not pleasant places to be but I felt safe and this for me was the turning point, I no longer had sole responsibility for myself – someone else was in charge. Through my treatment plan I came to the understanding that for me the idea of taking my own life was about control.

I had lived for so long amidst a maelstrom of emotions that I felt completely out of control and therefore suicide would have been the ultimate in taking charge of my own destiny. My key worker helped me to set realistic targets, initially very small, and to focus at the end of each day upon the positives that I had achieved as opposed to the negatives. I was assisted to evaluate my life and to plan for the time when I would no longer be working and have the social contact that my job provided.

Most importantly I was helped to see myself in a positive light and to come to the understanding that there are certain things in life over which we have no control and therefore have no culpability for. I have been well now for over five years, I still have odd days when I feel a black cloud lurking and it is then that I remember the seven Rs:

Recover your confidence.

Rebuild your life.

Rely on support and understanding.

Regain respect.

Restore your faith.

Rekindle your creativity.

Respect your beautiful mind.

My journey to good mental health has not been easy but I am a much stronger person for having undertaken it. I have been helped along the way by various professionals and some wonderful friends. I could not have done this alone.

Thank you for taking the time to read this and please do remember that whatever stage your journey is at you need not travel alone.

Best wishes,

Joseph

FROM JESS

Dear You,

You may be anxious, fears churning endlessly in your mind and belly, day and night. These thoughts are a false prophet of your future and of you. You will see the world differently too, in time.

You may hate yourself, for what you think you have done or who you think you are. Believe me, those who have loved you, love you still. You will know this to be true too, in time.

You may feel despair, will this hell never end? Listen, 'this' is only a bad dream. You will wake up to a better life too, in time.

You may feel numb, your emotions in a cold fog. This is only deep winter. Spring, summer and autumn lie ahead for you too, in time.

You may feel alone. Trust me you are not. Many stand next to you now, shoulder to shoulder in the darkness.

We are there but you cannot see us. Even more of us have been 'there', yet we have returned home. You will too, in time.

You will get better.

Jess

When managing depression the small moments of hope need to be counted.
Being able to smile a little, seeing some scenery you love, laughing at a TV programme.

FROM SUZANNE

Dear You,

I don't know if you'll be reading this because when I felt
like you do, I didn't read anything. I had tuned out into a
kind of dead zone where everything moved faster than I
did, it was like watching the world through glass.

I didn't know I was depressed because I thought
depression was all about crying, and it is for some
people. But for me it was a rift, a loss of connection, of
my capacity even to think, and of my most favourite
thing of all, my ability to dance. I remember the night
– getting up to weave and sway as was the style and
not being able to find the rhythm. I wasn't shocked or
distraught though, and this is the thing about some
sorts of depression, I was just foggily puzzled and I went
home. A bonus is that I was never suicidal, probably
because I just didn't have the ability to think enough
words for that, although if left on a beach with an
incoming tide, I may not have been able to think enough
words to escape either.

It was a good few years before that mojo came back but it did. In the meantime, I ran home from the bus stop if daylight broke before the bus arrived, did filing jobs that didn't bore me even though they would have bored absolutely anyone, plugged away like a barely animated zombie until one day, a small spark ignited somewhere. Just the tiniest light that grew brighter over the next months and slowly burned away the fog and cracked open the glass walls. I don't know where it came from any more than I know where the fog came from but there it was.

It's many years ago now but if this is you, I want you to know that the plugging away worked and that I didn't know I was working on my recovery because I didn't know I was recovering from something in the first place. I just discovered, with hindsight, that keeping going led to that spark, and the spark to a fire, and the fire to the colour and the music coming back. I still have the odd dark moment but that feels now more like a quick visit to the basement before getting back in the lift and cruising the upper floors again.

I'll never forget that vacuum or the emptiness it created, but it's made me who I am and I'm very happy with that person. So here's to long-haul zombie-plodding recoveries where you don't even have to know what you're doing to come out the other end. I'm wishing that for you now and every day from now on.

Suzanne

FROM TREVOR

Dear You,

I know you hate it when people tell you that they know what it's like to be depressed because they were once a bit sad when they lost their pet hamster. But they say they went for a run and soon they were back to normal, and if you just tried a bit harder you too could pull yourself together and snap out of it. I know you're insulted: do they tell people with cancer just to snap out of it? These people don't mean badly, but the world is full of them, and they won't help you at all. When you feel stronger you can put them right, but sometimes you will just have to ignore them. You only have so much strength.

Being severely, clinically depressed is nothing like being a bit sad. You don't want to do anything, you don't want to get out of bed, you just want to sleep, but your sleeping patterns are all messed up and you might spend all night staring at the clock, before feeling exhausted and dreadful the next day. You eat too much or you eat too little. You eat foods you know are bad for you. You have difficulty carrying out the basic maintenance jobs of life, and it depresses you even more as they pile up around you. Nothing gives you pleasure, and you can't imagine ever experiencing pleasure again. But being depressed isn't just an absence of pleasure: it's acutely painful. It feels like a red-hot knife being twisted in your soul. You sit in the dark and want to cry all the time and you think about death and what a relief that would be. People shouldn't have to endure this much pain, so you're not surprised that so many hurt or kill themselves. You will wonder about joining them – but please don't.

There will be many times when you think that it is completely hopeless and you feel like giving up. Then you need to remember two things. First, there are things you can do that really will help. See a professional if you haven't already. Get medicated (although remember that unfortunately antidepressants can take weeks to work). It took me years to get the medication right (or as right as I think it's going to be). Try and eat healthily and keep regular hours. Get fresh air, exercise and light. Keep to a routine. It will be difficult but there will be minor victories and it will stop you going lower, and perhaps even raise your mood. And most importantly of all, talk to people. One of the worst things about being depressed is the dreadful sense of loneliness, isolation and alienation it creates. Making contact will help you to remember that there are many others just like you – and some, unbelievably, worse off. Seek them out and talk to them. It's easier now with the internet – there are many blogs and forums that you can browse without what is sometimes the tremendous effort of leaving your chair. There are also many depression memoirs and biographies which will ease your sense of isolation and hopelessness. Read them, and you will see that others have after all been before to where you are now, and got out of that place.

Second, and most importantly, you must remember that all things pass. You will get better this time because you have in the past. It may take two months, it might even take longer, but eventually you will feel better again. It is easier to endure something if you know there's going to be an end, and there will be. Your past predicts your future. If this is your first bout of depression you don't have experience to help you, so listen to what others say. It's certainly my experience that I've always got better, and in my worst hours the belief that things will improve is the only thing that keeps me alive. So even if you just need to count seconds down, remember that eventually things won't be quite as bad. There might be a lot of bad seconds left, but seconds pass quickly. And when you are better again, you will appreciate how good things can be. When you've been looking at a monochrome world for a long time, a sudden splash of colour can be amazing.

Good luck.

Trevor

FROM JAMES

Dear You,

In the dark treacle of this illness it may seem impossible that you will ever be well. You may want to end your life, or hurt yourself or just stop feeling the unbearable pain of whatever has caused this.

It seems impossible that you will ever feel normal again, to feel like you did, to laugh or not think about the pain.

The loneliness of this illness is impossibly cruel, it may feel that no one understands how awful it is. Whereas no other person can completely follow the feelings and emotions you have, there are many others who have felt this dark and have come out again and live full lives. It is possible. With patience, care, rest and love you will get better, your body is telling you to stop, to climb off the horse and sit in the stable awhile.

Get help, push for help, you are important even if you don't feel it, remember people care and want you around, people love you and want you to live.

Hope is the one thing that is in short supply with depression and it is the one thing that we need when unwell.

I hope you continue to live, I hope you recover.

James

FROM JON

Dear You,

My name is Jon I'm a carpenter with a wife and two young children.

Two years ago I had depression; I don't know how long it lasted, maybe two years, but for the last year at least I thought about killing myself constantly (like, almost *every waking minute of the day*). I got so good at hiding it and 'coping' I used to play with the children while I had an image of myself hanging in front of my eyes.

I only realise now how ill I was. Recovery took a while and a lot of the time it felt like a lot of effort. Sometimes (while I was recovering) even feeling happier was too much to bear.

Two years down the line I can't actually remember much about it, it's just gone. I look at my kids every night and feel so blessed for the time I have with them, I'm enjoying my work again and my partner and I rarely go through a day without sharing a laugh. It's all very different.

I remember thinking, 'Why can't anybody see how much I'm suffering?' but I'm afraid they can't, you need to tell the people (even if the only person you can tell is your GP or Samaritans).

I went to my GP first and then was given a place on a group CBT course. I found this hard to cope with and was given one-to-one CBT and also started on antidepressants, both of which really worked for me.

I have just finished reading *Stop Thinking Start Living* by Richard Carlson. I am 100 per cent convinced by his approach to depression, his 'treatment' feels like cheating or a quick fix but it REALLY has worked for me. If you understand the principles behind CBT I think Carlson's approach could really work for you.

I'm still on antidepressants and I had a CBT group refresher last year. One day I'll come off the antidepressants but right here, right now, I'm happy.

I'm happy to be writing to you, I'm happy to be thinking of you and sending you my love.

You're not bad or unlovable, just ill. I'm holding your hand, I'll walk with you.

Yours sincerely

Jon

FROM ALISON

Dear You,

I don't have a 'typical' story to tell. And it might be safe to say that you don't either. Because there is no one experience, no textbook way to develop and live through these thoughts and feelings. But that doesn't mean your story, or mine, is any less than any others.

I had barely started my life when I wanted it to end and I have spent more years feeling depressed and anxious than I haven't. There is no defining trauma or event, no big change or alteration in my past that turned me from happy child without a care in the world to suicidal pre-teen anxious about just about everything. It crept up on me silently and took over me, changing me from the inside out.

Depression altered my perception of myself, my perception of others, and it defined and changed relationships with my family, my friends and the rest of the world.

Because I felt I had nothing to complain about, I hid my feelings for so many years, convinced I was in some way not able to justify how I felt and therefore not worthy of help and support. I was terrified of being called a melodramatic attention seeker, just a young privileged girl who was taking away time and resources from people who were in more need than I was. I lost so many years to a desperate sadness because I was convinced I was not worth helping.

But I have learned that I am. You are too. It doesn't matter what makes you feel the way you feel, you are justified in those feelings and you are worthy of being helped, worthy of being saved. I have never been more scared than when I lay myself bare, unleashed every awful raw emotion and finally asked for help. It took me nearly 15 years to do it and I don't regret it for a second. I only regret waiting so long.

When you're in the depths of depression, all there is around you is darkness. Little by little, the light you used to see is consumed by the dark. It shuts off pieces of you, sometimes slowly, sometimes all at once. And you'll forget what light is because you swear you've never seen it before. But I promise you, there will be light again. There will always be light.

These thoughts and feelings isolate you. They made me feel lost in a life I no longer knew how to navigate through, and I thought for the sake of others, I had to do it alone because I didn't understand who could love me like this. But I wish at those moments that someone had grabbed my hand and told me that I wasn't alone and that I was loved even if I couldn't feel it. And that is what I want to do for you, virtually grab your hand and tell you, you are never alone.

You are loved, so loved by the people around you, even if you cannot hear or feel it. I promise you it is there and will always be there. And there are so many people out in the world just waiting to meet you and love you as well. And when you get to the point in your recovery where you can hear and feel that love again, you will be overwhelmed by it. Slowly, you will learn to never doubt it again.

There is no one experience of struggling with your mental health and there is no one experience of recovery. I have tried many things to come out through the other side and I am still figuring it out. Some things work and some don't and that is okay. It's not easy, it's not quick, there are ups and there are downs. But I read once, and it stuck with me always, a Robert Frost quote that has helped me and may help you:

> In three words, I can sum up everything I have learned about life: it goes on.

Your past is not your present and your present is not your future.

I wish you strength, love, and above all else, a path out of your darkness and into your light.

Alison

FROM ZOE

Dear You,

I know things don't seem okay right now. I know you feel like giving up. I know how much that hurts. But I also know that it can get better. I know because I have been there too, and I am recovering.

I have always struggled with my mental health. I had an intimate relationship with sadness by the time I turned 13. Crying myself hoarse and lying awake for hours on end the night before a school day was a normal part of my bedtime routine. When I left home and moved to the city for college, it triggered a severe depression.

My depression was debilitating. I stopped eating, sleeping, showering, socialising. I stopped going to classes or turning in assignments on time. I stopped leaving my bedroom. Then I stopped getting out of bed.

Everyday life became a chore. I walked from point A to point B in a trance, paying no attention to traffic lights when I crossed the road.

I didn't care about my health, my education, or even my own life. I became numb. Like an empty shell washed up on the shore, I was sure that I was worthless.

My depression brought with it thoughts of self-harm and suicide. For years I had punished myself for signs of weakness and failure internally. I'd criticise myself for anything that made me stand out from my classmates, call myself names like 'stupid', 'loser' and 'idiot'. By the time I was 18 I needed to externalise that self-hatred. I started to hurt myself as a way of coping with the internal pain. I wanted to destroy the numbness. I wanted to make myself feel something.

Shortly before my 19th birthday I began treatment for my illness. I walked into the GP's office and said, 'I'm not okay.' Those were three of the hardest words I have ever had to say, but they changed my life.

My long, slow road to recovery began with counselling, psychiatry services and medication. Within a few months some of the symptoms of my depression became regulated. I could sleep and eat again. And in time, I slowly began to feel again.

At first, it was fleeting. A flash of a genuine smile when someone told a funny story. The warmth of another body when I was given a hug. A surge of worthiness when my mum said, 'I love you.'

And then I started to plan ahead. Marking a date in the diary for a concert that was months away, researching a post-graduate course and a possible career. For the first time in my life I could see some sort of a future ahead for me. I could see that I might actually live. Hope for a future sparked like electricity; I was slowly coming back to life.

Someday, you too will know that spark. It takes time, effort and a heck of a lot of tears, but it is possible. It is possible to feel, to live again.

Professional help didn't cure me. But it gave me something I hadn't had before: a chance. I had the chance to live, to find hope and to gain happiness. I will always have depression. I just won't always be depressed.

Yes, sometimes my depression is still hard to shake. It hasn't gone away. But I don't get lost in the thoughts and feelings of helplessness and hopelessness like I used to.

And I know now that there are steps that I can take to help me through my bad days. I've tried mindfulness, CBT, meditation, journalling, exercise, yoga... Not all of them worked. Not all of them will work for you either. But don't stop trying. Once I got that spark back, I never gave up trying again.

I graduated college. I got my post-graduate diploma. I got a job. And yet none of this had seemed possible before I sought help.

There will be days of joy and happiness. These days are more common than they used to be. And the days of being numb and hopeless are less frequent. Sometimes so infrequent that I expect they'll never come again.

So please, don't you give up. Ask for help. Try and try again until you find the magic that sparks you back to life.

With all my hope that you keep trying,

Zoe Alicia, 24

FROM STEVE

....

Dear You,

A sadness of the soul cannot be unwritten or un-felt in the moment.

Depression alone is a collection of states and 'definitives' proposed by others – try as we might, we cannot hide from it or deny it forever,

Sufferers don't become Tin-men or shadows, they still live,

Every man, woman and child may experience some degree of depression in their lives – be it brief, mutually felt or prolonged as soul-rending pain,

My pillow should not be made of misery, pain or torment,

Neither should yours!

End the societal stigma and frowning-faced denigration of others,

Before it ends thee, thou and we, when it is our turn to feel the burden of a heavy heart and mind,

Be kind to your fellow man,

Stop allowing people to suffer alone (or denying your own past pain and suffering, to 'maintain a good public image'),

Full stop! No ifs! No buts! No why should I's,

You would seek support too,

Do!

From Steve

FROM EMMA

Dear You,

Just now it feels awful, a pain you can barely comprehend, at other times so empty you feel like you have completely lost yourself. But I promise you there will come a time when you begin to piece yourself back together.

I know it feels like help isn't there, you've tried and tried and tried to find it and it feels like it is non-existent or you are not deserving enough.

You are important, you deserve help. Yes there may be people who are more ill than you, but that does not mean that you are undeserving of help.

You are loved more than you can imagine, people will not be better off without you, you are not a burden. That's the wee black monster talking, it is a convincing little bugger but it is a liar. Try and raise your head above the clouds and you'll feel the sun on your face.

Your friends and family are wonderful and they are there, waiting to help.

Stop smiling and pretending everything is okay – when your face hurts from putting on a smile, it means you shouldn't have been smiling. It is okay not to be okay.

You don't need to be strong for others all of the time, pretending you are fine isn't helpful. You have spent so long saying you are fine you have almost convinced yourself of your own lie. You are not well. Tell people. Tell people what you are thinking. Rip up the letter you have written and call someone or see someone, tell the truth. I promise you will feel better, it literally feels like a weight is lifted. You will no longer be carrying the pain on your own, others are there to lighten and help you carry the load. And the more people you speak to, the more the weight is spread, and eventually you will stop feeling it all of the time.

You are worth helping, you are loved, you are deserving and you can feel happiness again.

Love Emma xxx

FROM VICTORIA

Dear You,

I have been living and dealing with mental health problems for about four years but it wasn't until a year ago that I started properly opening up to people around me.

After some advice from my parents and teachers at school I agreed to get counselling in the hope that it would help me. Unfortunately, it hasn't worked as well as I hoped but let me tell you something, life for me right now has never been better. All of the support I received has taught me one simple thing: self-help is the best form of medication. I could carry on seeing my counsellor for the next decade or two of my life but, until I learned to stand on my own two feet, I would still feel exactly the same. This was my life, and only I had the power to change it.

To put things into perspective, I believe that recovering from a mental illness is the same as the birth of a butterfly. A caterpillar remains trapped inside a small, dark, claustrophobic cocoon until it learns to break free from its shell and grow into a beautiful butterfly. Once you start to face your mental illness head on, and properly begin the recovery process, you can finally spread your wings and fly. Prescription drugs and treatment might help you along the way, but ultimately it all comes down to you. Three words spring to mind: self-acceptance, self-help and self-love.

Another analogy that I love referring to is the idea that mental health problems are like clouds in the sky. Sometimes the clouds are stormy and consume your life, or you might even feel like you are lost in thick fog. And other times the sky might only have a few speckles of cloud, barely noticeable, but still there in the background. Clouds come, and go, and come, and go... It is important to accept that your life will have cloudy days every now and again. You just have to learn to dance in the rain, rather than simply waiting for the storm to pass. You might be having a thundery day today, but I promise you there will be sunshine eventually.

If you are suffering from depression, you have to embrace your illness and accept that it is only a temporary part of your life. Do not be afraid to speak out and ask for help. Sometimes you might feel all alone in the world but I promise there are people in your life who love and care about you. Do not think you are any less of a human being because you have to take medication in order to make it through the day. Do not let anyone tell you that you are weak. You are a wonderful and strong individual, with a fighter inside of you. You cannot let your mental health put you down or prevent you from doing what you want to do. Travel the world, meet new people, try new things. Make those around you happy, and you will feel happiness in return.

I know that the road to recovery is long and hard, but I promise you it will be worth it. There is a light at the end of the tunnel and, even if that light is merely a dim flicker in the distance, chase it. Chase the light and never look back. As Winston Churchill once said, 'If you are going through hell, keep going.' Accept your past and move onwards and upwards into the future. It sounds like a cliché but you only live once, and there is a huge difference between living your life and just merely being alive.

You get one chance to make your life amazing and we have to make the most of every single opportunity. So one day, when your life flashes back before your eyes, make every second worth watching.

All my love,

Victoria

FROM BARBARA C

Dear You,

I don't know exactly how you are feeling but I probably have some inkling.

I've had three 'breakdowns' in my life. The last one was by far the worst. I am over it now, I have been well for nearly three years, and you WILL get well again.

Matt Haig, in his wonderful, practical, easy-to-read-even-when-you-are-feeling-rubbish book *Reasons to Stay Alive*, says, 'Don't worry about the time you lose to despair. The time you will have afterwards has just doubled its value.' It is so true.

Try to say to yourself, frequently, that you have an illness, and when you are talking and thinking your negative stuff remember that it is the ILLNESS talking. It is not you.

Please try and eat well. To function properly your brain uses 20 per cent of your body's intake. If you are not taking in enough nutrients then your brain can't function properly. Try to think simple but healthy – all the usual recommended stuff – fresh fruit and veggies, sufficient protein and enough carbs. If you are anything like I was food was just not tasty or tempting. Never mind that – the adequate intake of sufficient food is vital to your recovery.

Everyone needs different stuff: my daughter when she was ill needed CBT, medication and small tasks to do that made her feel she had fulfilled something. I needed fresh air, exercise, masses of rest and – oddly – Sudoku puzzles. For a while I also needed someone to cook for me – my brain couldn't cope with the complex tasks of shopping and cooking, and I had a complete inability to manage the puzzling task of sorting out the recycling!

You may or may not find the medical profession helpful. I didn't, but that's not to say you won't. I found them unhelpful, judgemental, and determined that the medication – of which there were several different ones over the years – would solve the problem. For me it didn't. I pretty much gave up on the docs.

There's a school of thought that talks of the individual as a seed, planted in life's garden and trying to grow to its full potential. Sometimes, it seems, we have to develop a 'survival' self to cope, and we might end up living on automatic pilot. Crisis, in terms of depression or a breakdown, gives us the chance to rethink our learned patterns, and provides us with the opportunity to return to that self we were meant to be.

I don't know if you have a faith, i.e. a belief in God or a higher power. You might like to think about going to church. There are some brilliant churches around these days, full of bright, lively people who don't spend their time doing flowers and sewing cassocks, but are there helping people like you and me to cope and come to a better place in our lives. And they won't try and brainwash you. But you may just find the fact of being in a community with kind, gentle people helpful and life-affirming. It's worth a try, and the singing these days is magic.

Another book you might like is *Black Rainbow: How Words Healed Me* by Rachel Kelly. It tells of the writer's journey through depression, and how reading poetry helped her.

Please, try not to despair, you will recover – and your life will be so much more fulfilling than it ever was before you were ill.

With love,

Barbara C x

Recovery from depression
has no magic recipe, but
acceptance, love and learning
are part of the ingredients.

FROM B. L.

· ·

Dear You,

I want to begin by apologising for everything you have been through that has led you to this point in life. No one deserves to be hurt, abused, abandoned or made to feel worthless, useless and unwanted. Please know that while you may feel all alone in this world, you are not. I, too, have suffered immensely in life and struggled with mental illness. I can tell you, without a doubt, you are not alone.

I have walked the same path you are walking now. While our footsteps, our specific plights in life, may have been different, the journey is the same. I understand how you are feeling better than you could possibly imagine.

I understand how it feels to have trouble pulling yourself out of bed every day and to be in a constant battle with your own mind. I know how it feels to always want to cry, sometimes not even knowing why. I understand what it's like, as well, to walk that line between numbness and pain, where either everything hurts so badly that it's unbearable or you find yourself shutting down and feel absolutely nothing at all.

I know what it is like to feel alone, abandoned and discarded, that no one truly understands or cares. I understand the fear of opening up and letting anyone else in because you don't feel you can trust anyone. It is easier to isolate yourself than to have your heart shattered again.

I understand what it is like to feel broken and damaged, like a waste of space or mistake. I know what it is like to have others show and tell you so often that you are garbage that you eventually begin to believe it yourself. I also understand what it is like to question whether the world would be better off without you in it.

I know far too well that ledge we walk when things are at their roughest and we just want to give up. I understand completely that feeling of just wanting the pain to end, to just fade away and cease to exist. I have teetered on that edge a handful of times, though I have never fallen to my death. I am intimately familiar with that beast you are fighting. I know depression and its games well. Depression lies. It likes to shift everything to the absolute negative, leaving you to believe that NOBODY cares and NOTHING will ever get better. Depression wants you to lose all hope and faith because it wants you to give up. It wants to win.

Please believe me when I tell you that everything is not hopeless and the world is not lost. There is so much to live for in this world, so much to experience. You cannot succumb to its lies and let it win. You need to fight. I know it is scary to reach out for help because no one wants to be labelled as 'crazy', 'mental' or 'damaged'. Talking about all you have been through can be terrifying, at first, but once you pull your demons into the light, it is easier to face them and to heal.

You are so much stronger than you realise. You have survived so much in life. Whenever you feel weak, please take a look back at all you have overcome so far. If you could conquer all of that, there is nothing in this world you cannot face.

I cannot promise you that everything will one day be magically better, nor will I ever throw out tired clichés about clouds having silver linings or there being rainbows after the storm because I don't believe in empty promises or words. I can promise you, however, that you are not alone.

There are so many others out there struggling, too. We hear you. We understand. We feel your pain and we are here for you. You are never alone.

Please know, too, that the world needs you. Think about how you were feeling the moment before you began reading this, completely lost and alone, questioning whether continuing to live was even worth it. Somewhere out there, someone else is feeling that same way. All over the world, there are people suffering, struggling to hold on. All those people need us. We must do our best to reach out to one another, encourage each other, help each other back up when we fall.

We need to work together to be the voice of change. We need to find our voices and stand up to the stigma of mental illness. We must let those suffering know they are not alone, encourage them to reach out for help, inspire them to speak out and heal. You may have begun the day feeling worthless and inconsequential but you have the power to reach out to someone else and give them the strength to carry on and keep fighting. We all have that power. One by one, we can make a difference just by letting someone else know they are not alone.

Please stay strong and don't give up. Your trauma and abuses do not define you. Your mental illness does not define you, either. You are the sum of your actions. Look at all you have overcome. You are a survivor. It is time to take your voice back, speak out and heal. Do not let your depression win.

You have the power to be the voice of healing and change.

I believe in you.

Sincerely,

B. L. Acker

FROM ANNIE

Dear You,

I'm sorry you're hurting so much right now. I remember wanting to hear that. Wanting to die so the pain would stop and feeling so alone in that dark and desperate place.

It matters that you are in pain. It matters.

I want to tell you something that saved my life one night. I was planning to take my own life. To attempt suicide again and complete it this time. Except this time I searched the internet and I stumbled on some information that changed everything.

Suicide is not chosen. Suicide occurs when emotional pain exceeds resources for coping with pain. It's like a plastic shopping bag breaking because too much has been packed inside it. It's been filled with things that weigh too much, that take up too much space, so the plastic sags and strains and then the handles snap and break.

You can't just put everything back in the bag and keep going. You need to give some of it away, you need something else to carry it all in and you need someone to help you do that even just for a minute or an hour.

For these few minutes, let me be that person. Let me sit with you here and now and help you hold some of the weight of that unbearable pain.

I found help in a number of ways. Healing looks different for everyone. I stopped trying to make my abusive family into something it wasn't and started mourning for my lost childhood. I went to therapy and talked to crisis lines.

But the person who helped me most was me. Sounds impossible, right? But I helped myself by being more gentle with me, this person who was hurting and needed compassion. I started being kind to myself.

I found a therapist who believed suicidal feelings were not unreasonable, but not insurmountable either. I learned to treat those feelings like a faulty alarm going off in my head, warning me that my shopping bag was about to break and I needed to stop and find somewhere to put some of the things that were loaded up inside it.

When I want to die, it's because I'm hurting and I've run out of space for that pain.

Sometimes all I could do was find a way to get through the next five minutes or the next hour. But hours turned into days which turned into weeks and months.

Today, being alive feels okay. I've stopped wanting to die. I thought that was impossible. That the pain would never stop.

The way out of this is tough, and that's not fair. It's not fair that you're sitting here now, with an emotional burden that's too heavy to carry. It's not fair that you have to get through this when nobody should have to.

But it is possible. It is possible for life to not only be bearable, but joyful. Part of you believes that, even if it's just the tiniest part of you, which is why you're still here, reading this. However close you are to the edge, hope and healing are not impossible.

It's hard staying alive when you want to die. It's hard to be kind to yourself but sometimes the actions have to come first, before thoughts and feelings.

And it can get easier. There can be light in the darkest of places. Find a spark and hold onto it, because eventually it will turn into a flame.

Hold on. You're worth it. Hold on.

With love from,

Annie

FROM ELISA

Dear You,

You're not a failure. You're not a bad person. And you're not alone.

Right now you may not believe any of that, but read it again. And again. Powerful light exists in those truths.

I understand that the darkness feels so real. When I'm hit with depression, my first waking sensation is over-whelming dread, and I'm totally convinced that every day for the rest of my life is going to feel this bad. Even if a tiny part of my rational brain tells me that's absurd and not true, I simply cannot imagine a different kind of day or feeling.

It's a weird sort of existence, one that feels lifeless without being dead. I remember feeling that I didn't want to actually kill myself because that felt like too much effort...but I didn't want to be alive any more because that also felt like too much effort.

What fooled me and others for a long time is the fact that I've always been a happy and optimistic person.

Most people couldn't tell I was struggling – and I didn't admit it myself for a long time – because I still did good work and succeeded in going through a lot of motions. As I told surprised people later, I'm a highly functioning dysfunctional person. But inside I knew I was falling apart. Whatever the cause of your depression, hear this truth: your body is under attack, and your brain is taking a hit. There's no shame in getting help when you can't help yourself. Depression is a journey of peaks and valleys, so take advantage of ways to smooth the road.

Please tell someone you trust how you're feeling – even if you sound crazy in your own ears, people are kinder than you realise. Be gentle with yourself. Use whatever you think could possibly help even a little: wisely administered meds, compassionate talk therapy, healing prayer, healthy foods and supplements (I'm sold on omega-3s and vitamin D), hot baths, pedicures, daily walks, whatever. Buy yourself flowers. Listen to banjo music. Have dessert.

Eventually, when the right combination of tools comes together and you let time work its magic, light will slowly dawn. Eventually, you'll wake up in the morning and sense something closer to relief – maybe just a hint at first, like an air kiss. Eventually, you'll look back at the dark shadow but realise you're not walking in it any more. You'll be able to see and even celebrate the bright truth that you're still you, and you always were.

Sending you a big hug and a prayer,

Elisa

FROM KEITH

Dear You,

It won't take long before you know something is wrong. It will take time to admit it, and to seek guidance. From ignorance comes awareness, from awareness you can find help.

It feels like a pit, that's how I imagine it. Do you best to be aware, a good day can quickly turn sour. A wayward foot finds the edge of the pit, you trip, arms flailing in some desperate attempt to grab the ground but it's too late, and you fall in.

The bottom is dank and cold, permeating your clothes. As your eyes adjust you can see the damp walls, covered in slime and moist in the musty environment. The only sound is the occasional splash of a water droplet on the earth beneath.

Look up. How bad is this day? Sometimes you can reach the top and climb out. Other times it may be too high, way out of reach.

You can sleep. You know that sleep occasionally provides an escape, not an answer, just a respite. Chances are you can reach up after waking and clamber out.

Seeking solace in the very things you think will numb the pain will only make that pain worse. As tempting as they seem, stay away from drink, don't smoke and resist drugs. The relief may be palpable but it's short lived.

Concentrate on the natural highs: exercise, good nutrition, meditation. These are the drugs that not only provide a high, but will help you stay out of the pit.

Remember, always remember this: no matter how deep the pit is, how many times you fall in, nor the distance to the top or the coldness down there, remember to be aware.

Realise you are down there and once you know that, remember you can always get out.

You can always escape.

Best.

Keith Foskett (Fozzie)

FROM CLAIRE

Dear You,

I have spent most of my adult life battling a depressive illness, from anxiety and panic attacks to deep-down low moods. It is an everyday battle for me. I have good days when I feel happy and the world looks promising but all too sudden a low mood can develop and I am again wondering why I am on this earth. Why I am suffering with an invisible illness that I don't wear on my face and people don't seem to understand. I feel alone, I feel a failure, worthless, these feelings are all too real with depression, I have been told it is not a sign of weakness but a sign that I have been strong for too long. That is certainly the case for me as I have been and am a carer for my family, I carry their burdens with my own, I think the depressive illness is an outlet.

On good days I believe my illness has made me the person I am today, it is certainly not an uncommon illness with many people suffering from it. On a day-to-day basis I am coping and living with my depression, you can too, you have to learn to love yourself and accept the fact that you are what you are. Unlike some people you may need some extra help, counselling or medication, there is no shame in seeking help, men or women alike, we all lose strength sometimes.

I have had counselling in the past and have recently been referred by my counsellor to IPT, which is interpersonal therapy, I am on the waiting list for it, I take Citalopram antidepressants but have also been on Prozac in the past. If you take any medication please keep up with it, it does help believe me.

Also, pets can be great therapy as they are non-judgemental. Even when you feel at your lowest and unable to face the world a cat or a dog can make you feel so much better, or any other pet you may have or like to have.

Hugs are also very nice from loved ones, even if like my mum who doesn't really understand my illness, a warm hug when I'm crying or feeling down means so much.

I hope within this letter I am giving you hope and the feeling of a warm hug because I would like to send you one, depression isn't anything to feel ashamed of, accept all the help that is available, ask your doctor, search for local resources, you don't have to suffer alone.

Also, find something you enjoy doing, no matter how trivial it seems, if it takes your mind off worrying or feeling down for just half an hour every day then it is worth it. Try to look after your health, be kind to yourself, I care for others more than myself but I have started to look after myself a little more.

Some days when I wake up with a low mood feeling worthless, I don't feel like getting out of my bed but I have a reason to, people that rely on me. I know that if you live alone you won't have that reason and you will feel isolated and alone. Getting out for a walk just seeing people or talking to someone can make all the difference to your day, there are plenty of groups you can join, or even some volunteering opportunities if you feel well enough to go out and be around people, I know it can be hard, back in 1995 I left the house, I was 21 and that was the year I was diagnosed with depression, it's been constant since then, panic attacks, obsessive compulsive disorder, anxiety, they have all manifested themselves over the years, I am 42 now, I feel a stronger person for it on good days but it's all too easy to feel worthless.

Please focus on all the positives in your life not the negatives; focus on things that have made you happy/do make you happy, leave the negative thoughts at the back of your mind, think of the things you have achieved even if they don't seem to be much, believe me they are, they are part of you, the person you are. I appreciate nature, the sound of a blackbird singing can make me smile, a little robin perched on my wall, pretty flowers, the sound of children laughing, the sun shining through my window making my skin feel warm. Focus on fun, even the silliest things, learn to laugh again.

I don't believe depression is curable but learning to live with it and manage it and knowing when to ask for help and not being afraid to ask for help is a cure in itself. Yes, maybe we feel different to other people but we aren't, the seemingly happiest person can be wearing a mask hiding their true feelings, we wear those masks well, that is why some people don't believe us and think depression is no such illness and an excuse. To live under a constant black cloud is not an excuse; we just have to find a way to forget it's there.

Within this letter I send you love and hope, you can live with depression, you can get through each day, be strong and never think of yourself as a failure because you are definitely not.

You are beautiful and you are alive for a reason.

Warm Hugs and Love X

Claire Young

FROM ELSIE

Dear You,

I have had more than my share of depression, and the last bout happened recently. Each time I knew at the back of my mind that the black hellhound would eventually pad away with its tail between its legs. The joker in the pack is that I did not know WHEN.

Depression for me was night after night of broken sleep, my head filled with thoughts of repetitive misery, sometimes with plans of self-destruction. Depression was booking a solo backpacking holiday and worrying that I would not get to Madeira at all because I would not have the energy to rise at four in the morning to catch the airport bus. Depression was needing to buy a pair of glasses with larger frames when my prescription changed and hating my reflection in the mirror. 'I'm old and horrible looking,' I said to myself, 'No one will find me attractive now.'

I'm not going to tell you that I feel happy right now because I do not want to bore or anger you.

What I will tell you is that when you are depressed your mind tells you lies. Everything is weighed down, darkened, distorted. You may feel that you are stuck this way for life. You are not. That is the depression talking.

My advice to you is simple – do what you can. If you have some work either paid or voluntary that you can continue with, that's fine. If you need to take time out or to leave, that's fine too, don't blame yourself. The same goes for any social life you may have. When I was depressed and I emerged from home to be with others I was tongue-tied and enjoyed myself less than before. I was a tortoise plodding on beneath my heavy shell, not a butterfly taking wing, but it was better than not going out at all.

Listening in bed to my favourite radio programmes felt warm and comforting. Depression for me was not a time of trying many new things, but it was a time when familiar routines helped the days and weeks go round.

You deserve better than this. Good things may happen when you least expect them.

Remember that woman with her new big glasses, staring into the mirror and thinking no one would want her? Eight months later I met an older man who I have become close to. He is warm and loving and grows the most delicious strawberries.

Wishing you all the very best,

Elsie. xx

FROM PRIYA

Dear You,

I know it. The nothingness.

I'm better now, so I can think about it like it was nihilism. But I know it wasn't. It was more physical than that.

I'd lie in bed feeling like I didn't know, couldn't think, what I could do to make this mental anguish stop. I felt nothing about my family, my friends, my life. I remember being in Morocco, with my sister. The pressure to feel excited, to feel, anything! But I couldn't. I curled into a lump and couldn't even cry.

You know what helped? Some pills, some doctors, some talking. Some friendships. And then life. Life took over. Things changed. In a way I could never predict. And now I feel alive again.

It can happen. That's what you need to hold on to That it can. That it will change again. And this thing that wasn't the depression, that you used to know as happiness, can happen, to you.

People can be good. Sunshine can feel good again. And once more, life.

Love, Priya

FROM KATIE

Dear You,

I see you.

I see you questioning it all.

I know they told you that 'some baby blues' is normal, but right now you are wondering what counts as hormonal baby blues and what is too much? You are wondering about those thoughts you have and questioning whether this whole 'have a baby' thing was a good idea. Maybe you weren't cut out to be a mom after all. Maybe you are wondering other things too. Things you are too afraid to say out loud.

I was there, Momma. Twice. And I am still here. And I see you.

The first time I found myself in that place, it took me nine months to reach out and get help. Too long. It was my first baby, and I knew things change when you add a baby to the mix, so I thought my feelings were normal. I thought the frustration, rage, overwhelming feelings and helplessness was just what it felt like to be a mom. I hated myself.

I started to dress in clothes I thought I deserved, now that I felt like a frumpy, worthless person: clothes I thought 'somebody's mother' would wear. Because I felt terrible about myself, I snapped at the people I loved the most: my husband and my mother. I called them awful names, told them they knew nothing about me or my son, and much worse. In short, I was verbally abusive.

That is also when I began having intrusive thoughts. I would be driving home from work on the highway and envision myself veering off the road into a tree at 80 mph (129 kph). I was starting to believe that maybe my husband and son would be happier without me. I loved them fiercely, but I just didn't believe I was a good wife or mother. I believed I was a failure. I hated myself and who I was and I attributed it all to being a mother.

After nine long months, my husband gently suggested I call my doctor. At that point I was too weak and beaten down by my own thoughts to argue. The next morning I made the call and was seen that same day.

I was diagnosed with postpartum depression (PPD) and anxiety. I would love to say that having a diagnosis and a prescription magically made everything better, but it did not. The fall into depression is fairly effortless; it just happens without permission or intention. The climb out, however, is incredibly intentional and arduous. It takes work every day.

Knowing what I was up against helped, though. I started taking an antidepressant and a few months later, I started therapy. Combined, they helped me find myself again; I realised that the intrusive thoughts were the depression lying to me. I was able to accumulate strategies to help not just cope during the times I stumbled, but also to see the pitfalls ahead and bolster myself rather than just hope it wouldn't happen.

Two years later, my husband and I decided to have another baby. This time I felt better prepared for what my postpartum brain would do. Unfortunately, it started while I was pregnant. My doctor had made the suggestion that I wean off my meds during pregnancy, which I tried to do. I was a train wreck of antenatal depression and it took extra rounds of therapy along with reintroducing my antidepressant to help me get stable again.

After my second son was born, I thought maybe I wouldn't experience PPD again, but as it turned out it reared its ugly head and pushed me into the pit again. This time I had a team of doctors and support surrounding me. We were ready. I was immediately re-examined by a psychiatrist who determined that I was also suffering from postpartum obsessive compulsive disorder and posttraumatic stress disorder from my first child and the previous miscarriages I suffered. Because of my previous experience with PPD, we were able to catch me before I fell all the way to the bottom of the pit. My medications were changed and I picked up new strategies and coping mechanisms from my therapist. I kept all communication open to my husband and the rest of my support team.

A year and a half ago I had our third child, a daughter. There has been no pit this time around.

While it would be nice to say, 'I'm cured!' that is not completely true. I am still on medication and I still see a therapist monthly. I still see the pits all around me. I know that I could easily fall into any of them at any time.

But now I have the tools to help me navigate a life full of pits. I know that some of those holes are deeper than others. I also know that some are so wide, I won't be able to go around them completely; I will have to go through them. I also know it's not a solitary endeavour. My family, my friends, my doctors are all with me helping me carry my burden, and even sometimes carrying me.

So I see you. You are in that deep pit right now.

But I'm here to tell you that you do not have to stay there. This is not your new permanent home, and you do not have to claw your way out alone. There are people out there willing to throw you a rope or even crawl in to that hole with you, to put you on their shoulders and lift you out.

I am one of those people. Hop up. It's time to get up and out.

Best wishes,

Katie Sluiter

FROM HANNAH

Dear You,

I promise you that this will go away. No matter what you tell yourself or even what others tell you...I promise that this pain and this exhausting ache to just survive will one day be just a terrible memory.

When you hear or read that depression never truly goes away, that is a lie. It can be overcome, and even though you might feel this pain again one day it is never as bad as it is now.

I sat in your position six months ago in a coffee shop reading through these recovery letters on the website and it was the first time in months I had felt anything. The only emotion I could feel was complete and utter relief to know that maybe this wouldn't last forever. And it didn't. Not even nearly.

I now wake up every morning and I get that lovely warm feeling when you don't want to get out of bed because of how cosy you are. I get excited when I find out that a lecture is cancelled because it means that I have an extra hour of free time to enjoy and savour. I look forward to the future, to seeing my family, to hearing from friends, to holidays. I remember a time when getting out of bed was a heavy, conscious effort and I had no future. Being around family and friends was even more painful than being alone because I had to pretend I was okay; I didn't just wish I wasn't with them, I wished I wasn't alive.

I am six months into my recovery and I know so much more about myself and everything! It's clichéd but it's true: it's the best thing that ever happened to me.

Wherever you are, and whoever you are, I love you and I am certain that this pain you are feeling is not permanent.

Even if you cannot remember what normal feels like right now you will feel it again soon.

Hannah

FROM BEN

Dear You,

I'm Ben I'm in my thirties.

Somehow. That fact surprises me in several ways.

I've tried to kill myself twice. Seriously. I've tried another four or five times, less seriously, more trying to get people to understand. I'm unsure on the number as overdoses have happened when I've been drunk, some of which I remember, some of which I don't.

Depression, I think, has been around me for most of my life, but it was given a name when I was 17. My dad killed himself. Unexpectedly.

I didn't talk.

I cried a bit for a day or two. But I was meant to be the strong one. I became distant from anybody and everybody. I drank, had fun and pretended everything was okay. I was a couple of months out from my exams, and got results expected of me, exceeded expectations really – nobody really wondered whether I was okay as the evidence was that I was fine; nothing to see here, move on please.

I didn't ask for help as I didn't think I needed help. I saw myself as an island. I was fine; when I wasn't then it was down to me to sort myself out, generally by trying to bury my head and plough on through. This changed after an abusive relationship, when I'd just wanted to die for what felt like forever and ploughing on through was getting me nowhere...

I've had psychiatrists, therapists (individual, group, CBT, psychoanalytic, existential, integrative, art, drama, dance and movement, Gonzo) and a whole host of others, but it took a while to get there. I've been amazed at the number of people who are able, willing and desire to talk about the inner depths of my mind and how much patience they will show me.

The idea that I could only be helped by specialists really played into the stigma I felt – was I really that messed up that only somebody who had years of training could help me. I stayed at a sanctuary for the suicidal in London (Maytree) and that really opened up the potential of being helped.

Life isn't a bed of roses now. Two years ago, I was suicidal on a daily basis. One year ago, I was suicidal on a weekly basis. Now, it's down to about once every few months. To some people, that may be scary and a bit strange. I like it; to a degree. It drags me down, but like a ball being dragged into the ocean, I bounce up higher. Depression and suicidal thoughts help me keep sharp. I accept it, finally, and that gives me a power over it.

I'm training to be a therapist now, or rather I am a therapist who also does some training. I feel privileged to have had my history as it means I can relate to people in a very un-theoretical way.

The stigma I'd felt was based on the assumption that the professionals are all sorted. They aren't, and from what I've seen, the better ones are those who know they aren't and realise they'll never be 'sorted' as it's a false aim. They cope and can understand difficulties; they don't think they're superior.

Depression has made me resilient – I can cope with so much as I know I've been there, done that and touched the bottom, and that's a springboard. It's also brought me a lot of friends and relationships that are founded on that level of honesty, and it's part of my relationships. My recovery isn't a denial of it ever happening, or a view that it won't happen again, but that things can get better. There are two phrases that really stick with me: 'this too shall pass' and 'amor fati' (which I have tattooed on my forearm). The latter means 'love your fate', but rather than viewing fate as this thing which controls me, it's about making decisions and choices today which give me the fate I want.

It isn't easy, but life isn't supposed to be easy, and I see my being suicidal as emphasising and really bringing the temporariness of life into very sharp focus.

Warm wishes,

Ben

Recovery is not about cure nor an end point, it's all about managing and living and reflecting and each day trying the best you can.

FROM DEBORAH

Dear You,

I am writing to share with you my unique experience with depression. You see, I know depression personally, and I know how to treat it professionally.

I didn't know it at the time, but depression was a big part of my life as a young girl. I was always tired and tearful and thought everyone felt those kinds of things. And no one – teachers, friends or family – took notice of my depression back in the 1960s. Partly because children weren't thought to experience clinical depression. Partly because I was able to use a smile to hide my pain.

The depression I experienced worsened as I got older, and when I was a teenager, it deepened to the point where I became suicidal. At age 19, I reached for a handgun to end my life. Luckily, my attempt was interrupted and I got immediate help. I soon learned from a therapist that I'd been struggling with the illness called dysthymia – and that it intensified into a double depression, where a major depressive episode co-occurs.

Together we made sense of why this illness was in my life. I learned about the science of mood disorders and how my genetics influenced this illness, how certain ways of thinking worsened depression – and ways to recover from this disorder.

I was so inspired by my therapy sessions that I became a psychologist so I could work with others who struggled with depression. It felt so empowering to take my personal experiences and apply them to the clinical knowledge I learned. With this unique perspective, I'm able to help many understand the textures of depression because I walk the walk and I talk the talk.

Personally, I understand what it's like having a mental illness. How you can feel betrayed by your own mind and body. I understand the shame that comes from needing antidepressant medication. And the frustration from side-effects. I know how hard it is to take the skills learned in therapy and apply them to real life.

I've also felt the cold hard stares and stigmatising remarks from others when they discovered I had depression. I remember a pharmacist once telling me when I called in for a refill, 'Yes, you can't forget to pick up your Prozac. There's a full moon out tonight.'

But I also know personally how following your treatment plan and getting support from loved ones can help you recover. I've sensed the moments when the illness starts to take a back seat, and then slips away in the background – no longer having a starring role in your life.

Living with depression helped me see what things are truly worth worrying about. How the small stuff simply isn't worth sweating over. In a way, the darkest moments in my life gave me an appreciation for finding happiness – and even joy. When you teeter on the brink of suicide, struggle with the physical pain of depression or the emotional corrosiveness of this disorder, you become resilient in ways that others never know.

Professionally, I know the kinds of treatments that work as well as the research that's out there on the subject of depression. I've seen hope appear in living colour as patients get better. I've watched as children and adults take techniques and conquer their depression. As a doctor, the one thing that is a must-do is to work your treatment plan with consistency. This is clinically called treatment adherence. Consistency doesn't just mean going to psychotherapy. Or taking your medication. Consistency means making every psychotherapy appointment. Being on time for sessions, and making sure you don't skip treatment because you want to go to the beach or just don't feel like talking. Consistency means taking your medication every day at the same time, with the same dose. Consistency means making sure you get refills in time so there's no break or gap in your medication regime. Treatment adherence means you aim to eat well, sleep well and exercise. That you make self-care a priority. As I doctor, I know this consistency is the holy grail – and as a patient, I struggled to find it. But once consistency is attained, recovery begins. And that's where the hope of feeling better becomes a reality. That's when you begin to be more than your illness. That's when you realise depression is a serious, but treatable disorder.

So, as you move forward, remember these two things that my unique perspective of depression offers:

As a doctor, I'm here to tell you there is hope.

And as a patient, I'm here to tell you there is healing.

Wishing you health and happiness,

Dr Deborah Serani

FROM KIM

Dear You,

I have, at various times in my life, sunk into a void of desolation.

Jokes are not funny any more, the future looks pitch black and the feeling of numbness is so intense as to be physically painful.

The stream of consciousness is so negative, but often the thoughts are not solid. Like they haven't fully formed in my mind. Just a background malaise of despair and self-loathing. I hate myself and the world around me.

The more time I spent dwelling the more depressed I would feel.

For me, what helps is to do stuff. Sometimes it doesn't matter what, just stuff. I just have to break out of that rumination cycle and keep persevering even when I felt utterly deflated.

There are times when I just don't care any more and I'll go the cinema in the daytime or find myself somewhere in nature. Other times I might find myself somewhere high up and even though I may have the thought that just one step off the ledge could end the pain, there is something about looking down on the world that gives me a higher perspective; makes my problems feel more insignificant and small.

At the worst of my depressive episodes I could see no point in living. Since then I've had experiences I just could not have imagined. Experiences I cherish. You never know what is just around the corner.

As I write this now I am skirting around the edges of depression, and I'm fairly certain through my life at points it will return. As far as is possible I endeavour not to think about these times as they simply feed the monster.

Depression can feel like a most feared enemy, especially if periods are intense and prolonged. I try to think of it as a teacher, and even as a healer. Sometimes when things are too much or I push myself too hard I need to feel Deep-Rest. In some way depression forces upon me a deep rest where I can see no point in anything any more. It makes me look at myself and my life and question whether I want to be living the way I am.

At points it has really helped me make changes that I would have been too scared to otherwise. I have seen many people through the process of depression and I can't help but feel it's actually trying to help us in some weird way; though it's tough to see it like this when I'm in it. Usually it's when things have improved that I can start to see the learning and try to build a more friendly relationship with depression.

Well, I hope you find something from these words that speaks to you.

Sending you my Best Wishes,

Kim

FROM IVY

Dear You,

I'm writing this letter to tell you that, if you're suffering from a postpartum mood disorder, you will recover and this is not your fault. I am writing to you to share my postpartum depression (PPD) experience with you. I hope that some of what I share will resonate with you.

They say that pregnancy and motherhood are characterised by these words: happy and glowing. But motherhood is not always happy. Motherhood is the toughest job you'll ever have, especially when you don't have any/enough support. When you go into it not knowing what to expect, it's only natural to feel anxious that you're doing a good job as a new mom. It doesn't help when PPD shows up at your door uninvited.

My journey to motherhood was not particularly happy and I seldom glowed. By the time I got pregnant, I was weary from all the shots and the anxiety from the IVF cycles I had to go through. It was a fairly smooth pregnancy except for the perpetual nausea that plagued me from beginning to end, the anxiety that carried over from all the failed attempts to conceive, and then the car accident that totalled my car and resulted in the loss of one of my two foetuses. Once my daughter was born, they had to remove my uterus due to placenta accreta, a rare condition in which the placenta grows into the uterus. I lost a ton of blood during the surgery to remove my uterus. During my week-long stay in the hospital, I was never allowed to sleep for periods longer than a couple hours at a time, I was never allowed to eat more than ice cubes, and on top of it all, I had to stay strong to try my best at breastfeeding even though I was separated from my daughter for much of the time due to my surgical procedure and recovery. I had to hold it all together, even though I was devastated that I could no longer have any more children.

Then, in the weeks after the baby was born, my daughter developed colic, eczema and cradle cap. I'm sure the anxiety that I was giving my baby a really bad start to her life contributed to PPD rearing its ugly head. I needed, but did not receive, reassurance that I wasn't failing as a mother for letting my daughter suffer from colic, eczema and cradle cap so bad that she went from a full head of hair to no hair at all. I needed, but did not receive, in-person support, like a relative, friend, support group or therapist. I had no online support, like Facebook groups and blogs. Nowadays, there are SO MANY Facebook groups and blogs. All you need to do is do a Google search and you will find them. My blog comes right up when you use these words: 'postpartum insomnia', 'can't sleep after childbirth', etc.

A week after my baby's colic ended, my PPD journey began. It started with insomnia and was followed by panic attacks, weight loss, loss of appetite, and inability to do anything or think clearly. It was clear I needed help and quickly. Had I not sought medical help, I'm not sure if I would be here today. Even though my doctor had an awful bedside manner, he did prescribe the right combination of medication that helped me recover. But the lack of bedside manner and lack of emotional support contributed greatly to the painful experience I was going through at the time.

From the time my insomnia started and my panic attacks were under way, and before I started to see a doctor for these alarming and mysterious symptoms, I had no idea that what I was going through was PPD. I thought I was losing my mind. There were times in which I wished I could disappear so I wouldn't have to suffer the way I was suffering. At times, I didn't think I was going to make it.

It wasn't until there was actually a name for my frightening experience that I was finally able to see a light at the end of the dark and painful tunnel. It's thanks to my ignorance that I lived in a state of fear. Once there was knowledge, there was hope!

Had I known then what I know now...or better yet, if someone had explained to me, before my baby was born, what PPD was, why it happens, and what to look out for, I would NOT have travelled that long, lonely and dark road during those dreadful weeks. I would have known that insomnia at six weeks postpartum is a common, initial sign of PPD. I would've known to ask my doctor (if he didn't already do so) to screen me for PPD and help me find the right help if he couldn't offer me any himself, rather than merely prescribing sleeping pills, shrugging off my insomnia, and saying all new parents are tired beyond words for the first few months. I would have also recognised other PPD symptoms like loss of appetite and rapid weight loss. I would NOT have been as scared as I felt as to why I had insomnia and couldn't sleep, even when the baby slept, and even though I was exhausted. My fear would not have escalated into panic attacks. I would have enjoyed my baby more in the first few months. I can never get that lost time back.

They say it's common for moms with PPD to feel like they are trapped in a dark tunnel with no exit and no light at the end of it. No one, not even my husband, knew the extent to which I suffered. No one understood how I felt because everyone said I looked fine, but tired, as all new parents look. It doesn't help that mothers do such a good job of hiding our pain behind a façade of smiles because society expects us to be happy. It doesn't help that only those who've experienced a mood disorder can truly understand what it's like to suffer from a mood disorder. Everyone else just doesn't get it, even though they may try to.

If you feel overwhelmed or feel like something is not quite right, or both, don't stay silent. Reach out. It's okay to feel overwhelmed by EVERYTHING and to need and ask for emotional support. Don't keep your feelings to yourself. Don't let feelings of isolation grab a hold of you. Your experience can make you feel ashamed and alone. But you are not alone. There are so many other moms that are, right now, going through what you are going through. There are those around you who can help, both in person and online, including other survivors, like me. Social support is critical to all new mothers. Don't go it alone. It really does take a village!

Despite all that I've gone through with my bumpy road to motherhood, I've become a much stronger person. As crazy as it may sound, I have no regrets over my experience. Had it not been for my PPD experience, I would not be the person I am today. I've become more confident and more resilient in the face of day-to-day challenges because I've adopted this motto: If I survived PPD, I can survive most anything.

Warmly,

Ivy

FROM LINDA

························

Dear You,

I am trying to write this letter to you today, even though it hasn't been one of my better days. My mood is much better than it was when I was really low a few months ago, but it is still up and down.

Sometimes I take a few steps forwards: this week I felt that oddly familiar buzz again – I remembered the enthusiasm I used to have for life. But today it feels a bit like I've taken one step backwards. So I am not going to tell you everything is going to be fine on the road to recovery, because I know it can get a little bumpy at times.

Depression, for me, is not simply 'sadness' but an abject sense of despair. Many people who haven't experienced it do not get this. They don't understand what it is like to feel so awful that you can barely feel anything at all; to be so without hope that there is no point getting out of bed to face the day; to believe everyone else would be better off without the burden of having to cope with you. There are those who will tell you to pull yourself together when you can barely push your head off the pillow. They have no idea how a person can feel this way, suffer no daily cycle of painful thoughts and self-doubt, and they possess absolutely zero empathy for your abundance of both.

But I do know what it feels like. Oh yes I do.

So, I can tell you how I've got as far as I have and why I keep going.

I tried to get myself moving again a little bit at a time – taking small steps rather than attempting, and failing the high jump.

I have attempted to stop beating myself up about getting depressed. It is a fact of life – I still cannot do all the things I would like be able to do. I've had to learn to forgive myself for not being who I wanted to and always imagined I would be, but instead a different (and perhaps a better) person for experiencing depression.

I allowed myself to accept help from others, who remembered who I used to be, and assured me that this miserable, grey, excuse for an individual was not – as I had feared – the real me. They helped me to remember the things I used to enjoy, but had stopped doing. They showed me that I had simply forgotten who I was.

There was a long period when I believed that I no longer fitted in because I was different. Now I am just beginning to see how this might even be something to celebrate.

Today was tough. I was stressed out and felt the tears returning again. But now, as I write to you, I can see that this feeling is different – more like the sadness I used to feel from time to time than the black curtain of depression coming down again. And by putting my thoughts down on the page, I have managed to make some sense of where I am at now.

At the risk of sounding clichéd (there I go again, criticising myself) – tomorrow is indeed another day.

I hope that what I have written has made some sense to you.

You are in my thoughts always,

Linda

FROM ALAN

....

Dear You,

I'm just sitting for a while, thinking of you struggling under that cloud called depression.

I remember a time when it physically hurt to think or feel; I forgot everyone and everything that mattered; I couldn't get dressed and barely ate; and the dark, scarring days when my wife wasn't sure I would come home when she watched me wander away.

After a period of intense business stress, I fell steeply into the horrid pit, rapidly becoming centred around how bad I felt – and there wasn't part of me that didn't feel barren and exhausted. I wanted to sleep constantly, looking to escape the hurt that hunted me down, but my wild and cruel inner world kept me alert and panicked.

I had never felt so alone and disconnected, without the sustenance of hope. I didn't realise how *hope* enlivened me until it was gone and I was crippled by the gaping hole it left. My mind's eye was blinded as my worldview narrowed to contain only my pain. Time slowed, blurred, then disappeared as I became a pacing, staring ghost – a shell of a person, hardly able to make an imprint on the world; as if *I* had died but my body lingered and dragged itself around. I had transitioned from *living* to *existing*.

The whole world would stalk me in the murderous arena of my deformed perception. Cruel ideas took shape from menacing shadows, taking turns bullying their way deep inside me – bursting through the door of my thoughts. I fought using every weapon I knew to keep them out, but they would relentlessly charge in, gouging at my raw, wounded heart *with knives sharpened on the stones of my faults and failings.*

Bizarrely, even objects like the mower, or the ceiling, could poisonously manifest and deform me with fear and self-loathing. I woke into the nightmare inside my private torture chamber for many months, moving in and out of a delirious, pain-relieving numbness.

The dreadful distortion grew so twisted and toxic that dying looked like freedom – both for me and my loved ones. My 'life' was wrecking theirs, adding another suffocating layer of emotional torment. Relentless pain overwhelmed the primal drive to live and I longed to let the death that had infected me lead me to its desired end – not *just* for myself, but for the others in my life. I truly believed *that ending my life would give them theirs back.*

I felt repulsed by, yet intoxicatingly drawn towards this false act of grace. As wrong as it seems now, it was so clear then. Thoughts of death were paradoxically comforting *and* terrifying. I researched and entertained suicide and often dreamt of dying – which felt like bliss, because there I felt nothing. I recall thinking many times that if there was a button that would stop the pain forever, I would have pushed it.

I am thankful suicide isn't that easy as I would not be writing this now or getting to see my children grow up. My first grandchild was born this year and two of my children got married. The idea that I could have disturbed and dishonoured the future of those I love tears at my soul.

I am so thankful just to be alive.

I had (or thought I had) severe side-effects to any prescribed medication, so I stopped quickly. While mentally incapable of engaging talking therapies – because concentrating physically hurt and non-destructive thinking was impossible – my recovery was slowed. Much time passed before I could talk things through, or map a way out of the darkness.

As I reflect, I vaguely remember a gentle *letting go of the pressure to get well and the self-hatred* that joined me in the pit. Acknowledging that getting well was a process and to *stop fighting so hard* – with myself – relieved internal tension. As I released the pressure, it freed up energy to take small steps towards light and life.

Like being in a train that crossed a border while I slept, the turning point seemed to happen mysteriously deep inside me, rising to my awareness as I noticed the fog lifting and sensed the faint warmth of dawn. A tingling spark of life was lit. I then woke one day with the realisation that I had strangely, but palpably, crossed again the border between *existing* and *living*. It still intrigues me how *nothing changed, yet everything changed.*

As I rose, colours literally brightened, vision sharpened and I began to see that my destructive, life-sucking perceptions were not real or true. I slowly learnt that my thoughts and feelings were not ME.

Just like stepping back from an object helps appreciate it better, so I found that learning to find space within where I could kindly 'watch' the happenings of my heart, mind and body helped form a clearer picture of reality and identity. My long-suffering and brave wife, my family, friends, nature, diet changes, movement and many other factors helped nourish me. I also made radical changes to my work life and I am excited to have much still to learn.

Self-care feels guilty sometimes and foreign often, particularly practising mental health 'hygiene'. Watching thoughts come (with feelings on-board) and just observing them with interest remains delicately challenging. Like being on the platform of a train station, watching a train come in – a train of thought if you like – and choosing to notice it, instead of jumping on-board and going round and round getting nowhere useful.

I learnt too that the pain within depression wanted to grow into some sort of wisdom – and sensing that swirling wisdom tasted sweet. Embracing what the future REALLY holds (instead of what I imagined) brings a warm joy that helps meld what I/we have been through into the bigger picture of life.

Many things help a little and together they can help a lot. The thing is to keep putting one foot in front of the other and to keep breathing. Focus what energy you have on choices in front of you that represent positive or active ways to cope. Do your best to take little steps away from coping mechanisms that are negative or passive.

Remember that this point, or any point in time, is not where you will be forever – even though it may feel that way.

Stay in the game friend – for your future self and the others in your life – and to enjoy the view that is coming around the corner.

Alan – husband and father

FROM NATHAN

Dear You,

I wish to begin by emphasising that everyone's depression is unique and there is no single 'right way' to reach a point where you begin to believe that recovery is possible. Nevertheless, depression has an extremely powerful voice – this is something on which everyone with experience of this illness can agree. And when it's at its loudest it drowns out and virtually eradicates any traces of joy, hope and pleasure you had once experienced.

For me, when I begin to struggle, even merely functioning becomes exhausting. My confidence and self-worth plummets, my anxiety sky-rockets and I am all-consumed by a cloud of negativity – each and every positive aspect of life is masked. The cyclical nature of my depression, anxiety and consequential contemplations of suicide has me believing that there is no way to escape the recurring pattern of thinking. But there is a way to escape.

The very fact that you find yourself reading this letter assures me that you hold some hope for the future – at present it may only be a minute fragment, a tiny shard of light, but it exists and shall continue to grow in intensity.

I've learnt that, especially during difficult times, I have to endeavour hard to verbalise, and indeed organise, the thoughts in my head with the aim of finding some form of rational assessment to escape the darkness. This takes time, but you yourself will soon begin to find and subsequently harness your own coping mechanisms and strategies for managing your mental wellbeing.

It has been said many times in recent years, but there is no limit to how much it should be emphasised – talking is key. A great many of us have campaigned to reduce the stigma levelled at those living with poor mental health. I fully believe making this rather fluid condition tangible – giving it a voice and beginning a conversation – is essential. You know all too well how painfully lonely depression can make one feel. However, you most certainly are not alone. This is something which truly becomes apparent when depression is normalised through communication. By reading this letter, you are playing a role in that communication and for this you should be very proud.

I have had a lengthy course of counselling and take a combination of medications to suppress my anxiety, raise my energy levels and manage my depression. Management is possible, as is achievement and success.

For around 18 months of my three years at university I had very frequent periods of illness. My tutors were very supportive and I was reassured by the support network that surrounded me.

Help is out there and you do not have to face it alone. I graduated with a first-class degree – this was always the goal, but at times it seemed impossible. It wasn't. I have focused some energy since on creating a blog loosely based on mental health, but commenting too on current affairs – my career ambition is to work in some capacity within the field of journalism, ideally TV news production/broadcasting; so never lose sight of your dreams and let yourself celebrate your achievements (scale, type, impact notwithstanding). Set attainable goals for yourself and break everything down into small, logical steps. As you progress I promise you your confidence will grow and your capability to see past the low-hanging black clouds will increase.

If you take just one thing from reading this letter to you, let it be this: you have absolutely no reason to be, nor should you feel, ashamed for living with poor mental health.

You are not weak, you are not useless and you are certainly not alone.

You have much to offer and slowly but surely, be it day by day, hour by hour, or even minute by minute, it will get better.

Believe not only in yourself, but too in the many, many people who are there to help.

Sending you love, support and wishing you well,

Nathan

FROM BILL

Dear You,

Who knows why we suffer as we do? Nature, nurture, a combination? Guess it really doesn't matter, because we are where we are and need to play the cards we've been dealt.

I've spent the vast majority of my sixty-plus years on the planet managing an anxiety disorder and anxiety-related depression. And that includes years of self-medicating with alcohol. I'm now 32 years sober. I've worn your shoes. I get it. And have all of the respect and empathy in the world for you.

Several decades ago, I thought it was all over for me – my goose cooked. But as I now know, it sure as heck wasn't. Thank God I didn't throw in the towel, and, believe me, there were times when I was close.

All is not lost, my friend. It never is.

Continue to move forward, keep learning, be creative, take care of your body and psyche, and never, ever give up.

You Matter...

Bill White

FROM HUGH

Dear You,

I don't know you, but I feel close to you nevertheless, for the struggles that we have in common – and that's why I want to share my story with you.

Through my twenties, I suffered from a mixture of depression and anxiety in various ratios. The trigger was a difficult first job out of university: an unpleasant, bullying office atmosphere laid bare the lack of self-confidence, and sense of being a joke figure, that nagged at me throughout my childhood and teens.

I then changed career, to become a journalist, but my mental troubles followed me – and in fact increased. In particular, they intensified when it came to my career: I found myself agonising over every article I wrote, however small, and drinking excessively to numb the panic. A number of times I contemplated suicide. On one occasion, my housemate came home to find me with a bunch of paracetamol in my hand, moist with my saliva after I had stuck them in my mouth, before deciding against swallowing them. On another occasion, I went into work with the firm knowledge that I was going to die that day. As I remember, I found something perversely amusing about the fact, that at a lunch with colleagues, they were exchanging everyday small talk with me without knowing that this was the last time they would see me.

And yet, seven years on from that supposed last lunch, I am here and I am thriving – and sometimes I look back and can't believe how far I've come. My job is no longer a source of stress but of joy. I cherish my close friendships more than ever, and, most importantly of all, I dearly love and value myself – for all that I can annoy myself too! Meanwhile, over the last few years, the further along I have travelled on the road to recovery, the more I have been able to reflect on my mental health problems with the benefit of distance – and based on that, here are five bits of advice that I hope may help in some small way:

1. Don't be ashamed of your depression. You know what one of the worst things about depression was, I found? The vicious cycle of feeling depressed about being depressed; I equated my poor mental health with being a poor person full stop. But now with hindsight, I can see that the aspects of my personality that contributed to my depression are also, from another perspective, qualities that I should be proud of. My anxiety over my job, for example, came from wanting to be the best writer that I can be – something, that now I have

a handle on it, is a very positive drive to have. And my wider depression came, as with you I expect, from thinking and feeling so much – too much, perhaps, but what does that make us if not highly sensitive, thoughtful individuals? And who would not rather be that than an insensitive, thoughtless person? Indeed, as I learnt to accept my weakness and not be ashamed of it, that was exactly when I began to get better.

2. Depression ain't all bad. That may sound like ridiculous wishful thinking to you, but honestly, if I could go back and relive my twenties without my mental health problems, I wouldn't. I couldn't honestly wish them away, knowing how they have, in the end, benefited me – primarily by helping me to become a more open, upfront person, with friends, family and the world. Earlier this year, I wrote an article for the newspaper I work for discussing LGBT mental health in relation to my own problems; here I am chewing over the subject again. And these are experiences I'd never want to have taken away from me; to share in our vulnerabilities is to be human, and thrillingly so.

3. Don't be afraid to dig deep. Depression is a chemical imbalance that cannot be explained away neatly. But there are factors specific to your life that contribute to it, of course, and taking the time to genuinely soul-search about those – rather than get stuck in that vicious cycle of being depressed about being depressed – can be really productive. In my case, I realised that a lot of the feelings of inadequacy that fed into my depression

were to do with my failure to come to terms with being gay, despite being notionally 'out' through my twenties. Admitting that I was uncomfortable with my sexuality made me, ironically, more comfortable with it, and was a huge step in my recovery.

4. There's no such thing as '100 per cent better'. Depression is not something you ever get over completely – and it's healthier to admit that to yourself, I think, than attempt to close the door and say, 'Hurrah! That's it, I'm cured.' I have wobbles now and then, but because I know that I am susceptible to them, they don't come as a shock, and I know to administer lots of self-care to deal with them.

5. Remember: 'We're all mad here.' That famous quote from *Alice in Wonderland* is one I carry round with me, literally – it used to grace the front door of a houseshare I lived in during my twenties, and I now have it tattooed on my back. It's a reminder to me that there is no such thing as 'normal' but also of how many people I know have also experienced mental health problems and the beauty, for all the sadness, that comes with sharing in that.

Finally, I just want to wish you all the very best.

It definitely gets better.

Lots of love,

Hugh

FROM MEGAN

Dear You,

Struggling with depression is one of the closest things a human being can endure to being stuck in time.

I'm sharing these thoughts from experience. It has been a journey I once kept contained within myself; one that I never thought I would even begin to understand, let alone gain the understanding of those close to me. The day I closed my eyes to the light and woke in the darkness was a day I was convinced that I'd lost myself completely.

How do you even begin to make sense of it when your life suddenly pauses and you find yourself stuck within an infinite stretch of nothingness; watching everyone around you carry on with their lives, running towards the future while you are left behind? That numbness you just can't seem to comprehend, slowly replacing the oxygen you once breathed in, poisoning your bloodstream the more you struggle for air. The sadness you can't shift, lurking around every corner you turn and echoing its cries through each painful movement your body tries to make. That vicious hum of anxious energy that strikes time and time again when you have your back turned, potent enough to stop your heart mid-pulse and cruel enough to leave you hanging there until you are convinced it will be the last beat it will ever sing.

That desperate search to track down the glimmer that was once yourself becomes a one-way road that always leads you back to where you first started. After a few effortful attempts running down the same path over and over again, you eventually find yourself getting more and more exhausted with every step you take; until your mind and your body begin to run on an empty soul; a dried-up motor that rusts and cracks under the heat. Depression for me was a never-ending moment in time, one which I thought I'd never escape from.

One of my first therapists – one of many to follow – gave me some valuable recovery advice back then which has stayed with me to this day. He said to me, 'There is a clear difference between believing that you can't, and knowing that you can't.'

When I heard those words, my perspective finally shifted enough to stop myself from running down that same one path. The reason why I had stalled in this endless loop of despair and a tunnel vision of doom was because I had made myself believe that recovery wasn't an option for me. But in reality? The opportunity to get better was there. My eyes just couldn't shift the fog that was my own damned perspective.

And then all of a sudden, the possibility of recovery became real. It was as simple as getting out of my head and remembering where I was – more importantly who I was – at that very moment.

So to you dear friend, please remember this. The next time you feel like you are stuck in time, the truth is: you are not. It only feels like you are stuck there. Remind yourself that outside that perspective of yours, the clock really is ticking away. And it's leading you to discover the most breathtaking, most beautiful opportunities you thought you could only dream of before now.

Hold on for hope, recovery begins with you.

Love,

Megan

FROM RACHEL

Dear You,

I hope you got some sleep. If you didn't, I hope you're resting, and can find the focus to get through these few lines. If you don't feel up to it right now, you can always come back later. This letter will still be here, waiting for you. I will be patient with you, but you must be patient with yourself, too. Just three short years ago, I was in a very similar place to you.

Sometimes, three years feels like no time at all. Other times, my depression feels like it was in another life. Often, it feels like it is just around a corner, and I might stumble back into it, like a familiar side street I had somehow forgotten how to find, but that my muscle memory has brought me back to.

I won't say I found myself in the exact same place as you, because your pain is different.

Everyone's pain is different, and it's important to remember that.

But it's also important to remember we can, at the very least, listen to one another and bear witness to one another's pain. Someone else knowing, even if they can't completely understand, is a start. 'I think I'm depressed.' Three years ago, I forced the words out. I was frightened.

'Would you like me to prescribe you something?' was the immediate response, before I could even draw in a new breath. The doctor was impassive, seemingly unaware that the words I had just spoken felt like they had been torn from my chest.

I paused, attempting to collect myself.

'I think I'd rather try something else first.'

'Are you having money trouble?'

I'm vaguely confused now. No, I am not having money trouble. I am having Trouble, with a capital T. I am somehow in a place where I can't actually feel like an active participant in my own life.

I went to counselling, for a year, then took some time off and then, maybe one of the braver things I have done, went back to counselling again. I admitted that I wasn't entirely better and looked for the energy to carry on with the hard work of getting to know myself.

Depression is a fight worth finishing.

One day, doing things for yourself won't feel so pointless and shameful.

One day, you won't have to work so hard at reminding yourself that you are deserving of small comforts, and big comforts.

You deserve to exist. You deserve to have a space to call your own. You deserve time, and love and patience. You just need to give those things to yourself, and the rest will follow.

There are a lot of us out there, fighting hard to keep depression under control. One of the biggest lies depression tells you is that you're alone. You're not.

Be well,

Rachel

Hang on in there.

It gets better.

FROM JAKE

Dear You,

My name is Jake McManus, I'm 43 years old, married and work full time as an electrician.

I suffer from various types of mental illness, this ranges from being manic, super-motivated and feeling I can take on the world, to spending days hiding under the bedcovers afraid of the outside world or the intrusive thoughts of suicide which won't leave my brain. I can...

In fact I'm going to STOP right there!!!

I don't want to sound like an over-complicated victim, I don't want to hear how I'm a beautiful angel who can grow wings and fly, I'm not in a battle, I'm not in recovery and I'm certainly not defined as a person by one of the two hundred or so different diagnoses of mental illness.

I don't claim to possess a miracle cure   I can't promise you that everything will be alright...not today, next week or even next year, but I can tell you that in my experience nothing lasts forever, in time life can change and we can help ourselves by accepting 'who' and not 'what' we may believe we are.

When I was six years old my mum passed away unexpectedly, around the same time my best friend at school also passed away. I was lost, confused and on a downward spiral for many years to come. By the age of 14 I had a criminal record and I was increasingly confused and out of control. By the age of 19 I cared less about life than I did about death and I have a scar on my left wrist to remind me of this. I've just lifted my sleeve and stroked the scar but that particular pain left me a long time ago. I'm not ashamed of it, I don't hide it but by the same token I don't show it off. Many of us have mental or physical scars and at first glance these may appear to be self-inflicted but if we look deeper there is usually a reason behind our issues.

We can't always control what happens in our world but we can try to control how we move on from it.

A few years ago a very close friend committed suicide and my life seemed to change forever, in my mind I wasn't coming back from this... Three years on I was suffering from prolonged sleep deprivation, psychosis and anxiety and I was heavily medicated. I couldn't see any way out and at a loss I decided to give myself 365 days to live. I wrote a letter of intention to myself and fully intended to keep my promise when the final day arrived.

Somewhere along the way (and I can't remember where) I stopped worrying about if I was bipolar, delusional or any other label I had Googled for years. I realised that I had certain 'unfixable' problems which were beyond my control and so I stopped trying to fix them. I didn't realise at the time but a weight had been lifted from me. I started to take walks in the woods and I would wake up early in the morning to watch the sun rise when there wasn't anyone else around.

Eventually I had an impossible dream of climbing a mountain, I don't know why and I didn't know how. The thought of interacting and finding someone to teach me was far more worrying than the fear of falling but this was a tangible fear, not a nightmare dreamt up in my brain.

With only a handful of my 365 left I found myself at the top of a mountain, I made the impossible possible. In my elation and disbelief I confessed my mental illness history to my mountain guide, Tom, who didn't even blink an eye. It wasn't important to him that I had 'issues', what was important was that I wanted to climb a mountain and somehow I got there. That day I realised that sometimes our 'issues' only have as much importance as we allow them to have.

It isn't a crime to say, 'Hey, I'm struggling with life and I need help.' You may be surprised at how many people are unsurprised at this and are willing to help.

After climbing my mountain I decided to open up, I spoke to friends and family. I wrote a Facebook post which turned into a page, which turned into a website about climbing and depression, and eventually I even made a short film for the BBC.

My life isn't perfect...I'm not fixed...last week I felt suicidal because I had a bad haircut, at 3.00am this morning I had a panic attack and wanted to ring an ambulance... I accept that this is a part of my life but crucially it isn't who I am as a person, I'm Jake and...

...I'm still here.

Take care,

Jake

FROM ODHRÁN

Dear You,

Because you are depressed I don't need to sugar-coat this. You and I both know that depression is horrendous and my heart goes out to you.

I am writing to you because I want to reach out and give you a verbal hug. I'm sorry life has become so hard for you these days. I want you to know, whether you feel it or not, there are people who really do care about you and will help you to find your way through this dark and difficult place you are in. I know how hard life can get and I also know we as humans have amazing inner strength and resilience that we sometimes only realise from our darkest moments.

When I was depressed I felt tortured and believed that life as I knew it before depression was over forever. I was overcome with constant exhaustion and other physical symptoms like headaches, chest pain, agitation and insomnia. I lost complete interest in everything and the simplest of things felt impossible to do. I was plagued with self-critical thoughts, poor concentration, pessimism and hopelessness. I really believed that everything had gone wrong in my life and that the situation was irreversible. There were many black bleak days where all hope seemed to be gone. And as if the situation wasn't hard enough for me, I blamed myself for it all and was consumed with guilt and shame.

My day-to-day life became unrecognisable. I cried sometimes for hours on end and yawned constantly. Waking early in the morning and knowing I had a whole day ahead of me often overwhelmed me. I worried about how I would get through the day, how I would fill the time and how I would bear it all. And each day I experienced varying degrees of anxiety ranging from general tension and worry to total dread and panic. I found talking to people almost unbearable. I struggled to make the simplest of decisions. I kept thinking about death, and everyday things like eating and grooming seemed futile in the face of my existential terrors. Many days I felt totally disconnected from myself and others and felt dead inside.

The ability to say to myself, 'You know that's not true' was totally gone. I thought I'd never work again so in my mind I was living out scenarios of what life was going to be like without work, broke, homeless. These kinds of negative thoughts fuelled an image of a miserable, meaningless, unliveable future. I really believed my career was over and that everyone was pissed off with me because I was letting them down. On top of this I believed that how I was feeling was the real me and that

I'd just been pretending to myself for a long time and that this is what life is really like.

I couldn't see how I could ever feel better but I wanted to feel better and that's part of what kept me hanging on. My mantra was 'just this moment' as I tried to get through minute by minute, hour by hour, day by day. The emptiness, bleakness and dread were almost unbearable but I got through.

It took a lot of time and rest and medication to get me to the stage of recovery where I could see the bigger picture of what had happened and accept it but for a long time I was dumbstruck at finding myself in the middle of a major depressive episode and kept thinking how, why, how, why me, how? Around and around. I had the feeling that my life was falling apart in an irreparable way. It was extremely frightening.

Today I'm now in a much better place and now blog about recovering. My experience of recovery from depression is in direct contrast to the pessimism and bleakness of depression. Now I am able to get on with my life and I feel content and relaxed most days. I feel able to live and my energy, enthusiasm and interest have returned. I'm back at work and have resumed doing the things I enjoy. I can see clearly now how unwell I was and how this affected my whole self and life but my experience of recovering has actually been a wonderful life-affirming one.

My recovery mantra became 'wellbeing is a daily activity' and that's how I'm now trying to live my life (and still learning let it be said!). No matter how bleak or painful your struggle with depression is, you can get better.

You can recover.

You can get back to living a life that feels worthwhile, enjoyable and fulfilling.

You can experience feelings of calm, interest and restfulness again.

You can feel connected and close to others and enjoy socialising again.

You can be happy with yourself and your life.

You can recover.

It helped me so much to keep reminding myself that 'this is depression' as I so often slipped into believing the depressed me was the real me. How you are now is you when you are depressed, and when you get a handle on the depression (with the help and support of others – we're not superheroes!) you will start to see this more clearly and feel yourself again.

You can find a way through this. For every person who gets depressed, there is an individual path to recovery that works for them. Trust yourself. You can find YOUR way through depression and come to an easier, more comfortable, happier place in yourself.

You have what it takes and you are good enough.

You deserve it after all you've been through.

Go gently!

Odhrán Allen

FROM EMERALD

Dear You,

You've heard it a million times before, and I'm going to say it again: mental illness does not discriminate. It doesn't care how smart you are, how old you are, what your income level once was, or what degree you hold.

But we do care about those things. We all have expectations for ourselves.

Growing up, I typically met the goals I set for myself. I was a decent student and a pretty good athlete, and I had a lot of drive. I was addicted to affirmation, so I always strove to impress my coaches and mentors, and as an adult I became obsessed with impressing my bosses.

As my depression shifted over the years, for many years it took the form of self-motivation, which was fuelled by a belief that I needed to be perfect, or the best, in order to be worthy at all.

Throughout my twenties I was so driven to prove my value that I chose to work sixty- and eighty-hour weeks when my boss expected forty. A colleague once said, 'If Emerald hadn't been working for non-profits her whole life she would be a millionaire by now.' I took that comment to heart, and once I moved to the private sector I gave myself a year or two to get to that point. No longer held back by the shackles of a non-profit...that million-dollar cheque was inevitable.

Yet...it never came. Various bouts of depression came and stayed awhile over the years. Already sucked into a vortex of self-hatred and inadequacy, I was often triggered by my financial failure: a missed student loan payment would send me to the depths of despair, even visualising suicide. An unexpected credit card interest charge or a bounced cheque...suicide obsession. A declined credit card at the grocery store...straight to the car. Tears. Struggle not to drive off the road.

I had not hit the metric. I was supposed to be a millionaire, yet I was a bright, capable person with a bachelor's degree, amazing work experience, and $0.70 in the bank.

What I did not have perspective of is that people with a mental illness have so much stacked against them that to merely get by financially means you are as successful as a millionaire. Folks with a mental illness often lose more than one support at one time. When I was so sick that I needed inpatient treatment, I had to quit my job, move from Bali to America, and find the money to pay for treatment. I was unemployed, virtually homeless (fortunately I had family to stay with), and in major medical debt.

When you want to get your life back on track after a major mental breakdown, there are very few supports. Although society in general understands that having an appropriate job, commensurate with your skill level and interests, is vital to long-term wellness, there are still very few resources available to help with that. To be financially stable you need to be able to find a job consistent with your skill level, apply, interview well, show up and perform consistently. Getting a decent job is hard enough for a healthy person, and as you very well know, when we are in the trenches with our mental illness, even the simplest things about life are hard.

Nowadays I feel a great sense of pride every time I pay my monthly bills, rather than feeling great failure that I'm not on a list of '35 Richest Women Under 35'. My metric has moved to a much healthier place.

If you are struggling to get to where you want to be in your life, and you feel that your mental health is a major factor in this, know that you are not alone. We cannot get to where we want to be if we are not well first. Prioritise your health and wellness. I have found that long-term wellness does not happen overnight; it is a result of consistent self-care and prioritising my mental health before everything else.

If you just take things one day at a time and keep your mental health the number-one priority, one day you'll hit your metric...but for today, just have some patience with yourself. We've all been there.

Best wishes,

Emerald

FROM LIZA

Dear You,

Right now, your heart feels broken. You most probably loathe yourself and wish you hadn't been born.

You can't understand why you are so depressed and why it has happened to you. What have you done to deserve this, right?

Believe me. Nothing. It is what it is. No one chooses to be depressed. You've done nothing wrong, so try and stop blaming yourself. I understand the hatred and feeling of helplessness you feel. The utter despair. It's all part of this horrid illness. It hides behind curtains and stalks you. Just when you feel a bit better it attacks you again. It lingers for days, weeks and even months.

You can't believe you could ever get better. But you will in time.

Your doctor will suggest medication. Do it. They may not work straight away. You may again feel like, what's the point? But, these things take time. You will need to hang in there and try different ones. Keep moving forward because they will and do work. Striving for wellness is the best and most powerful thing you can do for yourself right now.

In your eyes life can never be the same ever again. You may feel ashamed, and worse, you may feel you will never be able to recover and be yourself again.

Medication is the key to everything. You will gradually notice a shift. Take that by the horns and don't let go whatever you do. Take the steps necessary to thrive. Go for little walks, make a cuppa tea and sit outside and soak in the sun. Meet a friend, whatever, just put one foot in front of the other, little by little, day by day.

I don't want you to be scared, it may seem completely overwhelming. But the best and most exciting news is. It gets better. The depression will lift and you will be back to the beautiful person you are.

You are probably laughing and telling me I am an idiot right now. I get it. I do. I'm here to tell you not to panic. You will look back on this episode and applaud yourself for getting through it. You are an incredibly strong amazing sensitive human being. You deserve to love and be loved.

Depression. Is what it is.

It will knock you down, but you can get up and defeat it.

Love Liza M. Brock

FROM CHRISSY

....

Dear You,

I just wanted you to know, you are not alone in this darkness that you're feeling right now.

It has taken over your life, despite all your efforts to fight it. I want you to know, depression is a huge beast and it can consume you. I know you are doing your best to make it through each day, but some days are tougher than others, the days where you cannot get out of bed. It takes all the will in the world to get up and get dressed and leave the house, when all you want to do is to hide under the covers forever. Not seeing or speaking to anyone for days on end is what you would choose every day if you could. You can't sleep all night, you toss and turn, you cry for no reason. Morning arrives and you want to hide under the covers and shut life out.

You cry at everything and anything, not just a few tears, but sobbing your little heart out, until your head hurts and there are no more tears to cry. You feel like you are going to go mad and no one will understand if you tell them how you feel. I want you to know, they will understand, they may even confess to suffering from depression in their lives.

You can't understand why you feel despair all the time, nothing brings you out of this darkness. Not the sun shining brightly outside, not the pretty flowers in bloom, not the sweet children happily running around. Nothing... It just won't go away and you have tried really hard to make it go away. You cannot understand when and why it started.

I just want you to know that everyone suffers from depression at some point in their lives, so don't feel like you are alone and no one will understand you. I want you to know it is nothing to be ashamed of or to feel guilty about and no it is not your fault. I want you to know that strong people who have been strong for so long can suffer from depression, because they are exhausted.

I think depression is the mind and body conspiring to make you stop in your tracks, slow down, re-evaluate your whole life. You will and can get out of this dark tunnel that seems to be never ending. I want you know there is hope and you will defeat this beast. Do you want to know how I know this? Because I am a survivor and I have survived this war with my mind, and I won in the end. She almost stripped me of my essences, my spark, my lust for life.

I want you to know, you can win too, like many before you and many after you.

It will take time, small steps, it's okay, as long as you move forward and keep moving forward.

Chrissy

FROM MAZ-RIE

Dear You,

Depression is a daily battle with those voices in your head that say you're worthless and that nobody will ever want you or love you, that no one will ever understand this struggle. You feel like there is no light at the end of the darkness.

Then comes the realisation that you can't continue on the route of self-destructive behaviour. You know deep inside that it rips you apart, from the inside out. You keep putting yourself in the same situation.

You just stay lost in the moments thinking, Why did I do that? Why did I destroy a friendship? Why didn't I seek help way before now? Why couldn't I ask friends and loved ones to help me?

There will be times when you are feeling so low all you want to do is run and hide. You will want to shut everything and everyone out of your life. There will be days when you don't want to even get out of bed.

There will be days when all you want to do is cry but that's okay. You will begin to learn that accepting the depression for what it is means you can move forward. You learn that asking for help isn't a sign of weakness but a sign of strength.

You begin to notice you are not the only person feeling like this, there are many thousands struggling each and every day. We are just ashamed to say it or admit to depression as we still see mental health as one of those subjects we shouldn't talk about. But the more we do talk about it, the more people we can help, including friends or loved ones suffering from it.

Recovery for me means taking it a day at a time. Learning how to deal with stress differently so not only does it help my depression, it will also help my chronic pain. Recovery helps you to see life is too short. We need love and friendships to get us through the hard times. It makes us believe we can achieve anything. We start to see a light at the end of the dark clouds that depression pulls over us.

Life is too short to struggle alone; learn to smile, laugh and dance in the rain again.

After all, we all need to feel the love from friends or family. It's not only our fight, it's all of us fighting this together.

We don't have to fight this alone.

Maz-Rie

An illness that tries
to kill you through lack
of hope is powerful.
But together we are
the antidote to depression.
Talk. Support. Rest.

THERE'S LIFE
IN LETTERS

G. Thomas Couser

Although I spent my whole academic career studying 'life writing', I became interested in letters only quite late in life, when I finally came to terms with documents I found in my father's closet after his death. I was in my late twenties when he died but the circumstances of his death – from treatment-resistant depression and grief over my mother's death from cancer – were such that I didn't feel ready to explore this archive until I was in my early sixties. At that time, the documents, mostly personal letters, enriched, even transformed, my understanding of him, especially of his premarital life, when most of them were written.

When I began to examine my father's letters, I was writing a memoir of him – impelled by my own unresolved grief – and I was primarily interested in them as biographical evidence, especially of phases of his life that I hadn't been privy to. In addition, I hoped they would give me access to a man I felt I never really knew and perhaps explain his otherwise mystifying sudden psychological disintegration. But eventually I came to value the letters for other reasons.

Personal letters tend to express emotion rather than to convey information or ideas. But they have important work to do, their own purposes and agendas. Rather than just 'communicating', they can *bond* parties already known to each other – friends, relatives, lovers. In one letter, one of my father's close male friends referred to what he called Dad's 'philosophy of friendship and its relation to correspondence', by which he meant my father's notion that letters allowed each writer to absorb and store the other's virtual presence, to invoke at times when their company and comfort was needed. So I came to value Dad's letters for the way they created and maintained strong connections to others he cared about. No longer bonding him to his friends, now they bond me to him through those other bonds.

Among the most precious are letters he wrote to my mother from the Pacific theatre of operations where he served as an officer in the US Navy during World War Two. They offer invaluable insight into the relation that engendered me and into my nuclear family – my father, my mother and my older sister – before I joined it. Though not written to me, nor about me, they now connect me to him and to my mother.

All of these correspondents are now dead, but their letters engage me in an ongoing relationship with them.

In their afterlife I find meaning for my present and future life. I am immensely grateful for this window into my father's life – and my own. I now think of letters not as mere 'evidence' of life, as biographical data, but as bits of life itself because through them intimate human relationships are enacted and performed.

The letters in this volume are quite different from those in my father's archive. They are not conventional private letters written from one person to an acquaintance. Nor are they 'open letters' written to a known addressee but made public to enhance their impact. Intended for publication, the recovery letters are certainly open. What distinguishes them is that they are intended for unspecified and unknown addressees: those whom they hail as respondents. The letters beckon to these addressees from a position of recovery, of relative wellbeing; they offer reassurance and encouragement. They invite their readers to imagine them as issuing from their own future selves. They thus attest to and enrich the still vital phenomenon of letter writing.

For all that we may think that letter writing is a lost or dying art, correspondence still flourishes in new media. Certainly, I write much more personal correspondence as email than I ever did as 'snail mail'. I am not troubled that my messages may never be printed or stored. It's important only that they are read and keep me connected to other people I value. They do this by implicitly characterising our relationship what they are understood to be, how much is invested in them. Indeed, the correspondence *enacts* these connections and constitutes our bond even in a seemingly evanescent medium.

Popular culture also provides evidence of the ongoing human need for correspondence. In the recent Spike Jonze film, *Her*, a firm called BeautifulHandwrittenLetters.com pays the protagonist handsomely to compose personal letters for clients. Ironically, his letters are not beautiful – his prose is quite pedestrian – nor are they even handwritten: he dictates them, then they're printed in cursive script and mailed. That the letters are ghost-written seems to be an open secret; their recipients are not fooled. Despite these ironies, I think Jonze intends a tribute to the enduring stature of the analogue letter and of handwriting itself, which should function as a sign and seal of authenticity, uniqueness and individuality. The film accords surprising respect to handwritten letters – even if that respect is tinged with misplaced nostalgia, as if they were obsolete. Even, or perhaps especially, in a post-postal world, people continue to value personal correspondence.

There are two significant aspects of old-fashioned correspondence. First, we have to wait for letters to arrive. This delay both defers gratification and heightens the pleasure of eventual fulfilment. Second, a letter's material insubstantiality – a couple of ounces – is disproportionate to its potential emotional effect, its power, which can be huge. My father's letters certainly were worth my waiting to get – first when I found them immediately after his death, fifty years after the earliest of them were written, and then several decades later, when I finally gave them my full attention. By giving me intimate access to my father, they helped me understand his depression and to moderate my own – enabling me to acknowledge both our temperamental similarities and our different histories. Perhaps not coincidentally, my only serious depressive episode occurred during the first years of my father's decline. I struggled through it without much in the way of relief from medication or therapy. Only later in life did I own my depression and seek treatment for myself. At that time, I was engaged in writing the memoir of my father, whose depression proved fatal. Reading his letters at that time was itself therapeutic. They continue to keep my father alive and in relationship with me. And I hope that the letters in this volume may help their readers to fend off depression and to see the value in their own lives.

. . . .

G. Thomas Couser is Professor of English emeritus at Hofstra University in New York, where he taught American literature and American Studies and founded and directed the Disability Studies Programme. Among his books are *Recovering Bodies: Illness, Disability, and Life Writing* (Madison, WI: University of Wisconsin Press, 1997), *Vulnerable Subjects: Ethics and Life Writing* (Ithaca, NY: Cornell University Press, 2004), *Signifying Bodies: Disability in Contemporary Life Writing* (Ann Arbor, MI: University of Michigan Press, 2009) and *Memoir: An Introduction* (New York: Oxford University Press, 2012). He has recently completed a memoir, *Letter to My Father: Recognition and Reconciliation*.